A Lion
Called Christian

❋

A Lion
Called Christian

Anthony Bourke and John Rendall

FOREWORD BY GEORGE ADAMSON

BROADWAY BOOKS

New York

Copyright © 1971, 2009 by Anthony Bourke and John Rendall

All Rights Reserved.

Published in the United States by Broadway Books, an imprint of
the Crown Publishing Group, a division of Random House, Inc.,
New York.

www.crownpublishing.com

BROADWAY BOOKS and the Broadway Books colophon are
trademarks of Random House, Inc.

Originally published in hardcover in Great Britain by Collins, London,
in 1971 and subsequently published in the United States by Doubleday
& Company, New York, in 1972. This revised edition published in
Great Britain by Transworld, a division of The Random House Croup,
Ltd. and is reprinted in the United States by Broadway Books, a
division of Random House, Inc., by arrangement with Anthony Bourke
and John Rendall.

Library of Congress Cataloging-in-Publication Data

Bourke, Anthony.

A lion called Christian / Anthony Bourke and John Rendall.

Originally published: London : Collins, 1971.

1. Lions—Biography. I. Rendall, John. II. Title.

QL795.L7B68 2008

599.757—dc22

2008044167

ISBN 978-0-7679-3237-0

PRINTED IN THE UNITED STATES OF AMERICA

London photos © Derek Cattani

Leith Hill-Africa photos © Born Free Foundation

(Photos by Derek Cattani)

Reunion and beyond photos © Born Free Foundation /
George Adamson Wildlife Preservation Trust

Book design by Chris Welch

Photo inserts designed by Tina Henderson

1 3 5 7 9 10 8 6 4 2

First Paperback Edition

TO CHRISTIAN AND OUR FAMILIES

WHO NEVER MET HIM.

Contents

CONTENTS

Acknowledgments

In the 1971 edition of *A Lion Called Christian* we thanked the people who had helped make Christian's life with us in England both possible and happy, and those who helped return him to the wild.

In London: Roy Hazle, the Buyer for the Pet Department at Harrods, and Sandy Lloyd; Jennifer-Mary Taylor, Joe Harding, and John Barnardiston, the owners of Sophistocat pine furniture shop on King's Road, where Christian lived in London;

Kay Dew; our accepting neighbors in the World's End; The Reverend H. R. and Mrs. Williamson and Joan and Rod Thomas at the Moravian Close; Christian's best friend, Unity Bevis-Jones, Amelia Nathan, and Bill Travers and Virginia McKenna, who introduced us to George Adamson.

In Nairobi: Monty Ruben, Jack Block, Agneta von Rosen, Ulf and Marianne Aschan, and the Ministry of Wildlife and Tourism, who agreed to Christian's rehabilitation at Kora.

At Kampi ya Simba, Kora, north of Garissa on the Tana River: George Adamson; his engineer and road-builder brother, Terence; Tony Fitzjohn, staff Stanley and Hamisi Farah; George's lifelong friends Nevil Baxendale and his son, Jonny (George's godson); the Provincial Game Warden of Garissa Ken Smith; veterinarian Dr. Sue Harthoorn, cameraman Simon Trevor, and the Tana River Council.

At Collins, the original publisher: Sir William Collins, and our then editor, Adrian House; Derek Cattani, for his photographs in England and Kenya;

and Toni Rendall and Mandy Barrett, who typed our original manuscript.

Sadly, some of these key people are no longer alive today, including Sir William Collins, George Adamson, and Bill Travers. George would have enjoyed the revival of interest in his work with lions and in Christian's life. The George Adamson Wildlife Preservation Trust continues to fund major conservation projects in George's memory.

Thanks also to Caroline Michel, Alexandra Henderson, Lauren Miller Cilento, Pat and Lindy Bourke, and Sally Gaminara for their help and advice in the production of this book.

Anthony ("Ace") Bourke
and John Rendall
2009

Foreword by George Adamson

In April 1970, I received a letter from London from my friend Bill Travers, telling me about "Christian," a fifth-generation European lion, and asking whether I would be prepared to take him over and rehabilitate him back to the wild of his forebears. The idea appealed to me greatly, not only because it would save Christian from a life-time of captivity, but also because it would be, in all probability, the first time an English lion had been returned to the life for which he was created.

I felt confident that his inherited knowledge and instincts would soon assert themselves, given the chance, and in spite of his breeding. I must admit that I did not feel the same confidence about his two owners, when I heard that they would accompany Christian and stay a few weeks at my camp. I was led to believe they were very "mod," with long hair and exotic clothing. My first sight at Nairobi Airport of pink bell-bottomed trousers and flowing locks did nothing to dispel my misgivings. But Ace and John soon restored my faith in the modern generation. Immediately, I sensed the bond of deep affection and trust between them and Christian. I know from experience how hard it must have been for them to leave Christian to face the inevitable dangers and hardships of a lion in the wild.

At the time of writing, Christian is nearly two years old. He is as much at home in this wilderness as if he had been born here. Apart from initial toughening-up, he required no training. Always

the wonderful store-house of inherited knowledge
has shown him the way.

George Adamson
Kampi ya Simba, Kora
15th July 1971

Introduction

In 1971 we wrote *A Lion Called Christian*, the story of a lion from London who returned to Africa. And now, forty years later, the Internet's YouTube has introduced a new world audience to Christian, an audience that is intrigued and enchanted by his extraordinary story.

We were two young travelers from Australia who had just arrived in London and unexpectedly bought a lion cub from Harrods Department Store.

We lived with him in London, then in the country, until it was arranged for him to be returned to Kenya and rehabilitated by George Adamson of *Born Free* fame.

Two documentaries, *The Lion from World's End* and *Christian the Lion,* were made about George Adamson assembling a pride of lions, centered on Christian's return to the wild. The YouTube clip features our unforgettable reunion with a now much bigger lion on our return to Kenya one year later in 1971.

This 2009 edition of the book is revised and updated. We are both proud of the 1971 edition, written when we were in our early twenties, and this edition is true to the original text. However, we took the opportunity to add new information and make some clarifications, and in some instances we have tried to express ourselves more effectively.

Forty years later, some of our memories are very vivid and some are vaguer. We have consulted two very good books referring to Christian which have been published subsequently: George Adamson's

1986 autobiography *My Pride and Joy*, and Adrian House's 1993 *The Great Safari: The Lives of George and Joy Adamson*. These books verified the chronology of some particular events for us and provided new information. Another source was the letters Ace wrote to his parents from this period that until recently he was unaware had been kept. The first edition of *A Lion Called Christian* concluded in 1970, and this new edition has been updated to include our visits to Christian in 1971 and in 1972.

This edition is in response to the great interest in Christian's story generated by the YouTube clip of our 1971 reunion. In April 2007 we began receiving e-mails alerting us that the reunion footage was on YouTube. We did not know who posted it, and we would not have known how to do it ourselves even if we had thought of it. We recently discovered that Lisa Williams, a young art student from Los Angeles, had posted the original footage (without any audio) in late 2006. We did not really monitor the interest, but in early 2008 we noticed the clip was becoming more popular. It was being sent around the world as one of those "send this on to someone you love" e-mails, complete with Whitney Houston's version of the highly emotive *I Will Always Love You* as the backing track, which had been added in 2007. The hits on YouTube began to climb into the millions, and other sites opened. We occasionally read the comments but felt like voyeurs into our own lives. Most people found the clip extremely moving and comments were very positive, which is apparently uncommon, and this was often remarked on by other commentators. It was a very special experience that we now all shared.

The Internet is unregulated territory, and quite a lot of the information about Christian and us was incorrect, particularly the suggestion that we were in danger when we went back to see Christian. George had now known Christian for a year, and he was confident Christian would recognize us and greet us, although he admitted later that he did not expect such an exuberant display of affection.

Late in 2008 the American television host Ellen DeGeneres showed the clip on her program and invited John and Virginia McKenna to appear. They were unavailable, but the showing of the reunion clip saw the hits on the site climb to three million and led to many other international television networks broadcasting it. Christian had become world news, and we stopped counting as the hits reached sixty million, and the sites expanded to over eight hundred. Hollywood producers began to call. Funny spoofs and parodies have since been posted, and another unknown person joined Christian to Facebook, and he now has many friends.

Christian's story was well known in 1971. The book was published in four languages and serialized in many magazines. The documentaries *The Lion at World's End* and *Christian the Lion* were repeatedly shown on television in many countries. Then, naturally, the interest gradually faded, and as the years passed the memory of the experience seemed to us like a secret dream, a fantasy, or even a hallucination.

Last time, in the early 1970s, people were aware of the entire story—the novelty of a London lion returning to Africa. But this time, because of those few filmed minutes of our 1971 reunion in the clip, the focus has been on the loving relationship we had with a rapidly growing, supposedly wild animal, and the extraordinary welcome we received from him after a year. The interest and the thoughtful responses have been overwhelming for us and have given us the opportunity to reflect on the experience so many years later. In an e-mail from Joanna C. Avery, she expressed that we were able to bridge the differences and stereotypes that society imposes on animals and reveal our similarities.

We have tried to understand why this story has struck such an emotional chord with millions of people. Is it the unconditional love Christian demonstrated? Is it about growing up and separation? Is it about loss and loneliness and the joy of reconnection? Are people projecting their own feelings and needs in relation to their own animals and the solace and companionship they provide? With the domination of technology and computer games replacing outdoor activities, are we all now too alienated from the natural world? Is it nostalgia for a time when childhood was more carefree and safer, with more freedom and time for youthful adventures?

The Internet has revolutionized communication and offers still-unimaginable opportunities for social networking and entertainment—information dissemination as well as social and political activism. Through the Internet we can now exert real influence on causes we believe in. We wonder what we could all achieve together if we work in concert to address some of the world's most urgent social, environmental, and wildlife issues.

A Lion
Called Christian

1

A Lion with a Price Tag

No zoo is complete without lions. The small zoo at Ilfracombe in Devon on the south coast of England was no exception, and the lion and lioness were a particularly handsome pair. The lion had been bought from the Rotterdam Zoo in Holland, and the lioness had come from the Biblical Zoo in Jerusalem. They had their first litter on August 12, 1969: four healthy cubs, one male and three females. Nine weeks later, with summer over and no more holiday crowds to attract, two female cubs were sent to an animal dealer and were subsequently bought by a circus. The remaining female and male were bought by Harrods, the Knightsbridge department store, and sent to London by train. The four cubs seemed destined, as their parents were, for a lifetime of frustration and confinement.

Three months before the cubs were born, we had left Australia for the first time, uncertain but optimistic. We had both graduated from university and had had a variety of jobs with no clear career path at that stage. We headed to London as many young Australians had before us, and well-known examples include the satirist Barry Humphries, journalist and broadcaster Clive James, academic and writer Germaine Greer, artists Sidney Nolan, Brett Whitely, and Martin Sharp, social commentator Richard Neville, and more recently, Kylie Minogue. Some Australians traveled overland through Asia and the Middle East, which is difficult if not impossible these days. We traveled independently for several months, but met up unexpectedly in London in late November 1969. We weren't exactly conscientious sightseers, but one day in an unusual burst of enthusiasm we visited, among other tourist destinations, the Tower of London. A suitable contrast, we decided, would be our first visit to Harrods. We were aware of Harrods' boast that they could provide anything at a price, of course. A friend had once inquired about a camel and been asked, "Would that be with one hump or two?" But Harrods seemed to have extended themselves beyond our imagination when, on wandering into their zoo on the second floor, we discovered two lion cubs in a small cage between the Siamese kittens and the old English sheepdogs. A lion cub with a price tag was not an easy thought to assimilate. The cubs were proving to be a successful drawing card for the Christmas shoppers, with the prospect of becoming the Christmas present for the person who already had everything.

We had not thought about lions before. Of course, we had seen them in zoos, but this was as far as our interest and knowledge extended. Neither of us had even read Joy Adamson's 1960 book *Born Free,* the story of Elsa the lioness. She had been found as a cub, raised and rehabilitated back into the wild by Joy and her husband George Adamson, who was a game warden with the Kenyan Wildlife Department. We sympathized with the cubs, for despite the efforts of the staff, they were incessantly disturbed by intrigued shoppers, yet we had to restrain the same urge within ourselves. Each person demanded a response.

The female snarled in an alarming manner and people were satisfied, but her brother pretended none of us existed. He was irresistible, and we sat, enchanted, beside their cage for hours.

John: "Why don't we buy him?"

Ace: "I've already named him Christian."

We found out much later that the staff had named him Marcus, a handsome masculine name, but

Christian seemed to suit him, and we liked the irony or joke about Christians being fed to the lions in Roman times, which was also a reminder of the danger to which we could be exposing ourselves and the people around us.

We intuitively knew that we were both serious, and a curious excitement began to grow. Even if it was only for a couple of months, surely we could offer him a better life than this, and try and ensure a better future for him. Or was it that we just wanted to take Christian away from everyone else and have him to ourselves? Neither of us had ever fantasised or dreamed about owning an exotic pet, but he was completely irresistible.

Suddenly our lives were to be incomplete without a lion cub. An impractical idea for two young Australians visiting Europe, but at least we could allow ourselves the luxury of investigating the possibility of buying him. We inquired if he was still for sale. The female had been sold, but the male was still available for two hundred and fifty guineas, equivalent in

2009 to three thousand five hundred English pounds. This was a vast sum to us, but undaunted, we nonchalantly agreed that it seemed a very reasonable price. The assistant at the zoo suggested we speak to the Harrods buyer. He was, she pointedly warned us, interviewing any prospective purchasers very thoroughly, as Harrods believed it was important the lions did not fall into irresponsible hands.

We returned the next morning looking far more respectable, with our hair skillfully flattened, and wearing the tweed sports coats our parents, very perceptively, had insisted would be useful abroad, but until now had been lying untouched at the bottom of our suitcases. We succeeded, with the help of a few tiny white lies and our enthusiasm, in convincing Roy Hazle, the buyer for Harrods, that we would be responsible guardians/foster parents for a lion. Now, when Harrods was prepared to part with him, we had the first option to buy Christian.

Everything up until this point seemed very natural and straightforward. We had gone shopping and had seen a lion that we liked and now wanted to buy, but could not take delivery for about three weeks. We shared a small flat on the King's Road in Chelsea, above the shop where we had both been offered work, and in all respects could not have been in a worse position to own any animal, least of all a lion. We spent days fruitlessly visiting estate agents, looking for a basement flat with a garden "for our dog." It seemed pointless being truthful with them when it was the landlords we would really have to contend with. We were becoming very disheartened, so we decided to advertise in *The Times* on the assumption that the courageous or eccentric landlord we had been unable to find would probably be a reader of this newspaper.

> LION CUB, 2 young men seek suitable garden /
> roof, flat / house London. 352-7252.

The only responses we received were a flood of telephone calls from other newspapers, prematurely wanting to photograph the lion.

In desperation, our last chance was to persuade

the owners of the shop where we worked, Joe Harding and John Barnardiston, and Jennifer-Mary Taylor, that in addition to us as employees, their business really needed a lion cub living on the premises, particularly as the shop was called Sophistocat. John Barnardiston was cautious by nature, being English, and fortunately he was in Switzerland at the time. Joe Harding was born in Kenya and had owned a variety of animals, and proved to be no opposition. And Jennifer-Mary was enthusiastic. It was decided that Christian would live in the basement of the shop, and it was to be a surprise for John on his return from Switzerland. As we would be living above the shop and working there, it seemed an ideal arrangement, for we could devote all the attention to Christian we realized would be necessary. Although Sophistocat had an enormous basement, with several rooms, we also needed to find a garden for his exercise.

Fortunately we had friends living in a studio only three hundred yards from the shop, with access to a most suitable garden. Fully enclosed, and covering three quarters of an acre, it is still owned by the Moravian Church. The minister was an ardent bird watcher, but not prejudiced against extending his zoological interests, he very generously gave his permission for us to use the garden. As a result, we now felt able to assure Harrods that we could fulfill the practical requirements for owning a lion in London.

Looking back now many years later, we should never have been allowed to buy a lion. We were naive about the risks and were without any insurance coverage. Since the enactment of the Endangered Species Act in 1973 in England, Harrods has no longer traded in exotic animals, and now have the Harrods "Pet Shop" as opposed to a "Zoo." We now appreciate how purchasing wild or exotic animals only encourages further trafficking in them.

But while our excitement accelerated, we became increasingly concerned by our total ignorance of the sort of problems that faced us. We had no realistic idea to what extent a lion could be domesticated, and we were aware that we could be taking on an impossible and futile task.

We had grown up in family households that loved animals, but this did not prepare us for what lay ahead.

Ace grew up in Newcastle, a city to the north of Sydney in New South Wales, Australia. He lived on the edge of the bush, rode horses, and always had dogs as pets, although at eleven years old he found his first cat in the vacant lot next door. There were many family camping and fishing holidays to the coast and into the country.

John grew up in Bathurst, a major country town 130 miles inland from Sydney, where the family pets included a number of tough Kelpie cattle dogs, cats, and often young kangaroos that had been rescued when their mothers had either been shot as vermin or killed on the road. Rabbits were also considered vermin, and along with their predator the fox they are examples of a disastrous importation of animals that have caused huge environmental damage to indigenous species and habitats in Australia.

At Harrods, we were told that the cubs had been handled by humans since birth, and that they both, particularly Christian, were responding to affection. (We were recently contacted by a former Zoo staff member who informed us that Christian's mother had rejected the cubs and she had hand-reared Christian and his sister.) Christian was the favorite, and appeared to have a delightful, even-tempered nature. As often as we could, we went to Harrods to play with the cubs when they were let out of their cage for an hour after closing time. We wanted to spend as much time with Christian as possible, and it would make his transition to Sophistocat and the King's Road easier if he was familiar with us. Both cubs were excessively playful, and while it was possible to handle them, they could be quite uncontrollable at times. They had extremely sharp teeth, and claws that they had not yet learned to control, and it was difficult to avoid being scratched. Christian was definitely more accepting than his sister, and we hoped he would be less boisterous and more manageable when he was separated from her.

Roy Hazle sensibly suggested that before we made our final decision to buy Christian, we talked to Charles Bewick and Peter Bowen, who had bought a puma from Harrods the year before. The puma was called Margot after a family friend, Dame Margot Fonteyn, the prima ballerina. She was now fully grown, and although she seemed to have adjusted to life in London, we never really felt at ease with her. We were assured that she had an impeccable behavior record, and because Peter and Charles had been able to devote considerable time to her, she was sufficiently domesticated to coexist quite happily with them. It was encouraging, for they had obviously found the whole experience enjoyable and much less complicated than they had anticipated.

We realized it was unlikely that we would be able to have Christian for more than about six months in London, and he would rapidly outgrow any environment we could provide. We were determined to make these months as happy and as safe as we possibly could for him, but was it fair if he was then to go back to a zoo? Surely this would just make it harder for him and the whole venture a marvelous indulgence for us. We decided to visit Longleat Safari Park in Wiltshire in the English countryside to see if it would be suitable for Christian. The park had opened in 1966, a partnership between the Marquis of Bath and Jimmy Chipperfield, the circus owner. This was the first safari park to open outside of Africa, and it was innovative in the care of animals but controversial at the time, as neighbors feared the lions might escape. We were aware that when it had first opened, basic assumptions about lions had proved incorrect, and the lions had suffered casualties. Now, with the park extending to over one hundred acres, and the lions divided into prides, the park owners appeared to have created the best living conditions for lions in England.

Roger Cawley, the manager, said he would be delighted to take Christian when he outgrew us.

Not only were we now in a position to have Christian, but we could also ensure that he would not spend the rest of his life in a zoo or in a circus. But still we both had very serious doubts. Were we really prepared to take on this enormous, binding responsibility? We could not ignore the fact that it was a lion, a basically wild animal and the most powerful predator after man, that we were bringing into our lives and the lives of the people around us. We knew that a workable human-lion relationship was not an impossibility, but we could not be certain that we would attain this with Christian. He was now four months old and growing very quickly. Soon he would be capable of inflicting considerable damage. But while one of us talked of our recklessness and the risks, the other spoke of the unforgettable and exciting experience that lay ahead. What finally united us was the staunch opposition from most people we knew to the idea of buying Christian.

Unwittingly, they intensified our determination to accept a challenge we might otherwise have resisted. Our parents were no doubt horrified, but only cautioned us against a decision we might regret, and that it would be difficult giving Christian up. It was a step into the unknown. We were young, we were looking for fun and adventure, and we had left Australia, our parents, and some of our inhibitions behind. It was the tail end of the historic 1960s and the beginning of the 1970s, times of great social change, optimism, and opportunities.

On December 15, 1969, we received a telephone call to say we could collect Christian unexpectedly a few days early because Christian and his sister had escaped into the adjoining carpet department in the middle of the night and destroyed some goatskin rugs that were part of a Christmas display. We collected Christian the next day, walking him out through the staff exit on a leash. The staff waved good-bye, no doubt relieved that their responsibilities were over. With Christian sitting majestically and deceptively still on the back seat of the car, we drove off toward the King's Road, extremely happy and nervously excited, but with an unvoiced suspicion and fear that we had committed ourselves to something that could prove just too big for us.

2

Sophistocat

It is a short drive from Harrods in Knightsbridge to Sophistocat in Chelsea, but after months in a cage, Christian's world must have suddenly assumed the most enormous proportions. Frightened and confused in the car, he scrambled all over us, and we had to stop frequently, having no idea how we could begin to control him. We tried to placate him with a huge teddy bear that we had bought him as a welcoming present, but his total lack of interest in it left us helpless. Eventually we arrived at Sophistocat, where friends waited impatiently. We carried him into the shop, and Christian, now much calmer, padded around investigating everything and cleverly evaded all the hands that tentatively and incredulously reached down to pat him. He seemed only mildly disoriented and focused most of his attention on us, for having played with him at Harrods after hours, we presumably represented the only link with his immediate past. We spent most of the night playing with him. Christian was ours.

A resident lion in the King's Road, Chelsea, was not too surprising. In the 1960s London had become a Mecca for designers, musicians, artists, photographers, writers, and many creative people and hangers-on, who were all part of "Swinging London." The Beatles, David Bowie, and the Rolling Stones were familiar sights around Chelsea. Fashion designers of the time included Mary Quant, Barbara Hulaniki at Biba, Zandra Rhodes, Ossie

Clarke, and Michael Fish. Exotic animals were part of this quite glamorous mix. In addition to Margot, the puma, we knew of a serval cat that lived nearby, while the casino owner John Aspinall kept tigers and gorillas. For a mile from Sloane Square, the King's Road was scattered with trendy clothes shops, restaurants, clubs, and antique markets. The façade was ephemeral, but the basic character remained the same—superficial and pretentious, but great fun and not without attraction. Every Saturday the road was blocked by a self-conscious parade of people and expensive cars. Tourists came to watch, while the others, in beautiful or flamboyant clothes, came to be watched. While the clothes were fun to wear at the time, in retrospect most of us were fashion victims, and we view the more recent revisiting of 1970s retro fashion with amused embarrassment.

Sophistocat sold antique pine furniture and was situated in a curious area called the World's End, which historically marked the point where King Charles II's Road and protection from highwaymen ended. A raffish tradition that lingered on. A long way down the King's Road, the World's End was becoming part of fashionable Chelsea, and the locals resented the growing intrusion of a few smart antique and clothes shops, which included Nigel Weymouth's Granny Takes a Trip and Vivienne Westwood and Malcolm McLaren's boutique then called Seditionaries, later Sex, and now World's End. Punk music and clothes would soon emerge from our grungier end of the King's Road.

Within two days Christian seemed to have fully adjusted to his new surroundings. Any initial inhibitions had vanished, and the teddy bear was already in a million pieces. He obviously enjoyed his greater freedom in this large two-level shop, and was much less boisterous without his sister. There was no indication that he missed her; perhaps we were some form of substitute, and having none of the indifference common to most cats, he wanted to be near us. Lions are not as disdainful as other cats, and are more doglike in their sociability. Lions simply *know* they are number one and just assume superiority. Now four months old, thirty pounds, and about two feet long, he was a larger-than-life teddy bear. He loved being carried and cuddled, and his paws would gently reach around our necks and his tongue lick our faces. He had soft, tawny-colored fur and was surprisingly heavily spotted. Although he was well coordinated, his paws, head, and ears were disproportionately large for the rest of his body, giving an indication of the size and strength of the animal he would grow into. But it was his beautiful, round, rust-colored eyes that dominated his appearance. He had a delightful, placid nature, and was so easy to manage that we felt we had over-dramatized the problems of owning a lion. He was even house-trained. With the fastidiousness of all cats, he and his sister had used the same corner of their cage at Harrods, so we were optimistic. In one of the rooms in the basement we had installed a heater and put blankets for him to sleep on. In a corner we placed an improvised lion-size kitty litter tray. After two days of making indiscriminate puddles and messes, which we followed each time by a smack and then carrying him to the tray, this problem was solved. He quickly learned his name, and "no." It all seemed too easy.

He was adaptable and responsive to routine. His day began about 8 A.M. when one of us came downstairs. Although it seemed unnatural, quite often he had to be woken, and a sleepy, blinking little lion would affectionately greet us and walk unsteadily over to squat on his tray. Then it was time to be fed. His first and last meals of the day were a mixture of baby foods: Complan, Farex, and milk, with Abidec drops for additional vitamins. Sandy Lloyd, the assistant at Harrods Zoo, had adored the cubs and looked after them extremely well, and she provided us with a carefully balanced diet for Christian. Two main meals, given to him late in the morning and in the early evening, consisted of three quarters of a pound of raw meat, a raw egg, and a spoonful of bone meal to prevent a calcium deficiency. We varied the meat and occasionally gave him an unskinned rabbit. Christian always carried the skin around Sophistocat for several days until it finally disintegrated or the smell was too overwhelming. And he enjoyed having huge bones to play with and gnaw, and as there was no competition from other animals, we could safely handle his food as he ate.

We were to find that people's preconceptions about lions were often proved wrong. For example, it is a fallacy that it is dangerous to give an animal such as a lion raw meat, which supposedly would turn them into "man-eaters." We rather enviously eyed the delicious fillet steaks that a French chef sometimes brought in for Christian. The chef loved lions and of course had access to plentiful supplies of meat. The quantity of meat Christian required increased weekly, and he became so expensive to feed that we regretted not making him a vegetarian!

He was inexhaustibly playful and had a variety of toys and rubber balls scattered all over the shop and in the basement. Wastepaper baskets were a great favorite, first to be worn on the head, totally obscuring his sight, and then ripped apart. We had to buy him hardy toys, for the average life of a normal teddy bear was about two minutes. He demanded our constant attention and it was impossible to ignore him. If one of us was reading a newspaper or on the telephone, Christian would immediately climb up onto his lap. Sophistocat was a jungle of furniture, and he incessantly stalked us through it, becoming expert at creating games. He knew we would not allow him to jump on us, but he would cleverly maneuver himself into a position behind a piece of furniture so that it appeared as if we were in fact temptingly hiding from him. Then with a clear conscience he would charge and leap at us. We developed a habit of glancing nervously over our shoulders. If we noticed him frozen in a crouched position with intent mischievous eyes, he would nonchalantly pretend to clean his paws, rather irritated that his fun had been spoiled, for the game was to stalk and catch us unawares. Very quickly we could usually predict what his intentions were from the expression in his eyes. He was always entertaining and amusing but very exhausting and demanding.

When we played with him we discouraged him from being too boisterous or over-excited, and we did not wrestle roughly with him or encourage him to chase us. We never let him realize the point at which he had become physically stronger than us and could harm us. We avoided and ignored any overt demonstrations of his superior strength. Sometimes while playing, if he had us in an awkward or dominant "alpha" position on the ground, he could instinctively sense his advantage and got a surge of energy and determination that would alarm us and seem to mystify him.

He looked forward each morning to the arrival of Kay Dew, the daily cleaner, for he was certain she had been provided for his enjoyment. He chased her brooms, rode on the vacuum cleaner, and stole or ate her dusters. She handled him very well, but warily watched the Farex and Complan smudges grow higher on the windows and glass doors.

When Christian first came to the King's Road, he was small enough to run around the shop with our customers. They rarely took seriously our initial warning, "Do you have any objection to lions?" One disbelieving woman, on seeing one of Christian's bones, said, "That bone is at least lion-sized." "That's what we tried to tell you—look behind you." She watched incredulously as Christian ambled past to claim his bone. Usually it was good for business, and the owners of Sophisticat were incredibly tolerant. Even the English had to react to a lion cub stretched out on the antique pine table they were contemplating buying. Most people were delighted, and no one complained about the occasional laddered stockings or torn trousers. Many women customers returned with skeptical husbands and friends, and carloads of children on Saturdays, which were busy anyway with the usual King's Road Parade. Sophistocat suddenly acquired an unwelcome zoo or circus-like atmosphere. To dispel this, Christian had to spend most of the day in the basement, and only the particularly disappointed, or the particularly attractive, could persuade us to take them downstairs to see him.

Every afternoon he went to the garden in the nearby Moravian Close for exercise. Harrods had given us a collar and leash for him, and while the collar looked incongruous, it was necessary as it made it easier to hold him, and he quickly forgot about it. At first we tried to walk him to the garden on his leash, as it was only three hundred yards away. But he never walked, just sprinted for a few yards and then resolutely sat down. He was frightened of the traffic, and people crowded around him. We dreaded meeting other animals, for although he did not appear very interested in them, they were still a diversion. For the first few weeks we could just pick him up and carry him, but he soon grew much heavier, and the short walk became an ordeal. While it would have been easier if he had walked on a leash, it was unfair to expect such unnatural behavior from a lion, so we did not persist, and resorted to driving him there in the car, or in the Sophistocat van. He was always manageable in both, but restless, as lions can never fully accept any form of restriction.

The garden was ideal. No humans, no animals, and it was surrounded by a high brick wall. This wall dates from the seventeenth-century Tudor period, and the present studios and the old Moravian chapel in the garden are built on the foundations of Sir Thomas More's stables. After a succession of eminent owners, Sir Hans Sloane sold the property in 1750 to Count Zinzendorf of Saxony, who bought the land to found a Moravian settlement in England. The Moravians, who were among the first independent Protestants, formed their brotherhood in 1457 when they protested against the moral corruption and political activity of the Roman Catholic Church in Bohemia. They take the name Moravians, rather than Bohemians, from the group of refugees from Moravia who settled on Count Zinzendorf's estate in Saxony in 1722. The Count's son, Christian Renatus, Count of Zinzendorf and Pottendorf, is buried in the garden. Actually it is a graveyard, but the Moravians bury their dead very unostentatiously—vertically, with modest horizontal headstones—so this was not at all obvious. Looking back, we do feel a little guilty about playing in a graveyard.

There was a large area of grass for Christian to play, and trees and hedges to hide behind. Interestingly, it took several weeks for him to adjust to all the space, and initially he would not go out into the center of the garden, away from the protection of the hedges. But then the garden became his established territory, and he adored it. He loved chasing and jumping on us, but we thought this was an inadvisable habit to encourage in a lion, so we kicked soccer balls for him to chase instead. He was remarkably fast, and beautifully coordinated. He would run after the ball, pounce on it, and dramatically roll over and over with it. The few times it snowed, he loved skidding through it and was not worried by the cold. We spent about an hour each day at the garden, which seemed adequate, for he was rarely reluctant to return to Sophistocat. Besides, it was time for his favorite entertainment.

Late in the afternoons, Christian would sit regally on the furniture in the shop window, in the spotlight and watch the activities of the World's End. He was the star attraction, and the people, particularly the children, loved him and were very proud of him. He seemed to belong to all of them. In the window he drew appreciative crowds of regular admirers or astonished newcomers. These were happy hours. If there were too many people and his view was obscured, he simply changed windows. Several motorists, seeing Christian unselfconsciously displaying himself, bumped into the cars in front. And a conversation was overheard between a child and his mother on a passing bus: "Mummy, there was a lion in that shop window!" "Don't be ridiculous. If you don't stop this lying, I'll get your father to thrash you."

3

Noblesse Oblige

We had not told Christian that he was a lion. We thought this knowledge would only lead to regrettable lionlike behavior. We avoided using the word *lion* in front of him, but occasionally had to spell out L-I-O-N to ignorant people, who thought Christian was a leopard because of his spots. He enjoyed looking at himself in the large mirrors at Sophistocat, so while he must have been confused as to what sort of animal he was, he knew exactly what he looked like. He often accompanied us in the car, and as there are possibly more sculptured lions in London than there are live ones in Africa, we decided to tell him the truth, before he discovered it himself and asked awkward questions. We drove him to Trafalgar Square to see the lions at the base of Nelson's Column. He was delighted to be such an obvious symbol of nobility. Fortunately, this information did not alter his behavior, for he had, like all cats, assumed superiority over us from the beginning. But too much knowledge could be dangerous or confusing, so we asked the Moravian minister not to tell Christian that the early Christians had been fed to the lions.

Consistent with their standards, Harrods had sold us a lion of quality. He was very healthy and had a beautiful nature. He was even-tempered, and not easily alarmed or frightened. These qualities were reinforced by his trust in us and his strong feeling of security. The fact that his behavior was, in general, quite predictable and consistent made living

The King's Road, Chelsea. Ace left, John right.

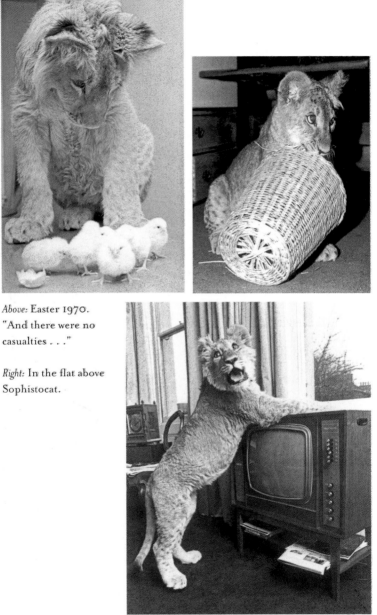

Above: Easter 1970. "And there were no casualties . . ."

Right: In the flat above Sophistocat.

Left: Surveying his kingdom in Sophistocat.

Center: His favorite position—on the stairs at Sophistocat.

Bottom: Football in the Moravian Close.

Right: Christian was always curious and could never resist an open drawer.

Bottom left: Christian, like all lions, was fascinated by children.

Bottom right: John (left) and Ace (right) with Christian on the stairs to the flat.

John (left) and Ace (right) in the showroom at Sophistocat.

Lunch with model Emma Breeze at the Casserole Restaurant in the King's Road, Chelsea.

Christian with Mark at Todd's Hairdressers in the World's End.

In the flat above Sophistocat.

Top: Radio presenter Jack de Manio tries to interview Christian, who failed to "roar" for the listeners, for the BBC.

Bottom: Christian meeting Virginia McKenna and Bill Travers in Sophistocat.

Watching out for customers at Sophistocat.

Playing hide-and-seek in the Moravian Close.

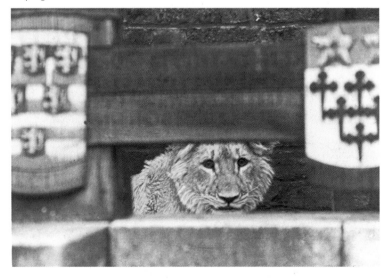

with him much easier than it could have been. We navigated our way very carefully with him, and learned about him quickly. We rarely misjudged his intentions, and we learned to anticipate any situations that could have unpredictable outcomes.

It was easy to recognize a psychological pattern of behavior in him that could be interpreted in human terms. While this is anthropomorphic, to us aspects of his personality did resemble a human's personality. His "sense of humor" seemed very similar to ours. If he tripped over something, and with his huge paws he tended to be rather clumsy for a lion, he appeared "embarrassed" but would quickly pretend, as most people do, that nothing had happened. It seemed lions can communicate with humans much more closely than almost all other animals can. We were realizing that the two most powerful predators in the world have so much in common.

Christian's personality was immense, and his presence entirely filled the shop and our lives. We realized that if the months he was to live with us were to be as happy for him as we intended, he had to be allowed as much natural expression as possible. For him to remain the content, even-tempered animal he was, it was necessary, in addition to giving him all the time and affection we had, to minimize any restriction.

We attained a relationship of mutual respect, with no hint from him of domestic-animal subservience. We made no attempt to dominate or train him, and in our experience this would probably have had disastrous consequences. Besides, it is doubtful if a lion can ever be totally dominated, perhaps just precariously controlled. And a lion's respect is not easily earned. Christian had a determined character, but he seemed to realize that he had to cooperate, and he quickly knew what sort of behavior would not be allowed. Neither of us has had any contact with circus animals or animals used in live entertainment. One can only guess at the psychological games, bribes, rewards, and punishments involved in getting animals to perform. In

2003 Roy, half of the Las Vegas double act Sieg-
fried and Roy, was attacked by a tiger during one of
their animal illusionist performances.

Christian hated being ignored, and was very con-
scious of the effect he had on people. He could not
resist testing the reactions of newcomers, and always remembered if people had not coped well with
him previously. Like all animals he always knew
when someone was uncomfortable around him,
and would take advantage of this. If customers had
not noticed him sitting on the stairs in the shop, he
would grunt to attract their attention. From this
commanding position, his paws knocked off several
hats and pairs of glasses. He was extremely curious,
and his eyes were always watching and searching for
anything new that had to be investigated.

It was his eyes that were his most arresting feature. They were expressive, intelligent eyes that could
transmit love and trust, or they could challenge or
defy us. Sometimes they had incredible clarity and
brightness, but sometimes they could be opaque,

unknowable, and impenetrable, and stare straight through us, beyond to a dimension from which we were excluded.

Christian possessed a memory for people and places, and demonstrated a high degree of intelligence compared to other lions we subsequently met. He quickly learned how to open the door of the basement if it was not locked. We kept his food for the day on the tops of various cupboards in the office at the back of the shop, and he frequently managed to cleverly climb high enough on other furniture, in order to stand up on his hind legs and knock his food to the floor.

Unlike most other members of the cat family, lions are gregarious and social animals living in an extended family pride. Christian undoubtedly regarded us as his family, and was tremendously affectionate toward us. Lions greet each other with a ceremonial touching of heads, and we often knelt to enable him to do this with us. Any parting from him, regardless of its duration, involved another fond greeting, a lick and a cuddle. He enjoyed being close, often either leaning against us or actually sitting on us. Sometimes he would dramatically leap from the ground into our arms, which was a greeting for us that no one had ever seen before with lions. Of course, he could be arrogant and demanding, but if he had to be disciplined, either verbally or with a smack, he accepted it and did not bear any resentment. He was very much aware if we were displeased with him, and if he felt it was deserved, he would make obvious and usually successful attempts to win us over again.

Christian was particularly unaggressive and unpossessive about his food, which indicated that in some respects he was an exceptional lion. He had no other animals to compete with and he was fed regularly, both of which must have been contributing factors. But people who knew a great deal more about lions than we did were always astounded by his attitude toward his food. He had a healthy appetite, and in his eagerness he often knocked his food out of our hands before we had time to place it on the floor for him. But we could take his food away from him if it was necessary, even out of his mouth. He loved the marrow inside bones, but as he was unable to get it out, he gently ate it from the tips of our fingers.

Lions depend to a large extent on their mouths for communication and contact. He licked us to show his affection. His rough tongue always tested surfaces for their taste and texture. He had sharp milk teeth, and while he enjoyed mouthing our hands and arms, he quickly learned not to bite us. There were moods, however, in which his mouth just hung open, waiting to be filled. Kneecaps were a suitable height. Our clothes were often damaged by his teeth or claws getting caught, and we sometimes resorted to wearing practical bottle-green boiler suits.

A lion needs to exercise his claws and jaws. In the first few weeks, several table and chair legs were damaged. However, after a few smacks he gave this up, especially when he realized he could use the banisters on the stairs in the shop instead. Lions are creatures of habit. They are earthbound in comparison with other cats, and he did not jump all over the furniture. But he enjoyed surveying his domain from a height, and would often sit on tables and chests of drawers. Fortunately, he preferred the stairs, which gave him greater height, and he would sit with a paw dangling elegantly over the side. Actually, he damaged very little furniture, and this only occurred if he slipped and dug his claws in for support. One day, rather unwisely, a very expensive table had been elaborately set with cutlery, china, glasses, and candles in the middle of the shop. We heard the sound of breaking glass and immediately knew what had happened. In the confusion Christian had moved his weight to one side of the table, and he and the tabletop crashed to the floor. The table had been sold, and now there were several deep scratches on it. We telephoned the woman who had bought it to apologize. "Don't worry," she said,

"I only came into the shop to see Christian. The table was an afterthought. Please don't worry about the scratches, they will remind me of that beautiful lion." But he could never resist attacking the mattress on a brass bed in the shop. This problem was solved only when a friend very generously brought Christian a mattress of his own and, wildly excited, like a wild lion with a kill, he expertly dragged it down to the basement, although it was much bigger and heavier than he was.

He had formidably sharp claws, and before he learned to control them, we received many scratches. But within two months he developed more control over them, and he also realized that we stopped playing with him if we were scratched. He learned to keep them sheathed, but if he was wrestling with something such as his mattress, pretending it was a zebra he had just stalked and thrown to the ground, we had to remember that his claws would instinctively be out.

Like all lions, Christian was fascinated by children and reacted differently to them, seeming to consider them a different species from adults. We were always extremely careful, and held him if children were in the shop. One day a photographer from a local newspaper was taking a photograph of him, on a leash, outside Sophistocat. A woman, probably thinking Christian was a dog, strode in front of him with her two-year-old child, also on a leash. Christian curiously extended one paw and knocked the child to the pavement. One of us grabbed Christian while the other obscured the photographer from the sort of photograph the newspapers crave. The child was slightly dazed, but so swaddled with clothes it could not possibly have been hurt. At first the mother was furious, but as she returned later with endless friends, and other children to dangle in front of Christian, she was apparently delighted with the incident.

But he grew very quickly. Within two months the beginnings of a mane developed and he suddenly looked quite adult. It was unfair, and probably unwise, to expect innocent customers to cope with a lion springing from behind a chest of drawers and clasping them around their thighs with his huge paws. He left most people alone, but like many other animals, he instinctively knew those who were frightened, and he enjoyed teasing them. Obviously, we could not risk any incidents, and no insurance company was prepared to cover us.

We began to feel the weight of the responsibility of owning Christian. Chelsea Football Ground is nearby, and the police visited us to advise us that on match days Christian should not be allowed to be in the windows as this could be a provocation to the passing football supporters. He had to spend much more time in the basement, and was only permitted in the shop when there were no customers. He enjoyed being there, and he had many toys to play with, but he resented not having the freedom to go up to the shop when he wished. Sometimes he would unnecessarily squat on his kitty litter tray, as an unsubtle sign that he was ready to go upstairs. Like all cats, lions are happy to sleep if there is nothing better to do, but his hours in the basement were broken by many visits. The others at Sophistocat—Joe, John, and Jennifer-Mary—adored Christian, and he was just as fond of them. Usually, at least one of us would be downstairs playing with him. When people came to see him, we took them down as it was easier for us to be in complete control of the situation, and, if necessary, prevent him from jumping on them. He was an unusually accepting lion and there were very few people he disliked. It was difficult to discover what he objected to. Sometimes it may have been a strong perfume or an aftershave lotion, and he always jumped up on one friend of ours, but only when he wore a particular coat.

We tried to keep him unaware of just how much, or how little, control we had over him. After the first few months it took him a surprisingly long time to realize that, although we could still just carry him, if he struggled we had to release him immediately. If he played too roughly with us, we stopped, and because of this, he never knew the point where he had, in fact, become physically stronger than we were. For a lion he was very obedient, and he usually cooperated with us. Only rarely would he ignore our remonstrations, and when this happened, there was very little we could do. We just had to pretend that we were not worried by what he was doing, rather than let him know that we could not stop him. It was a fascinating psychological game, but the stakes were high.

Lions give extremely clear and fair warnings of their displeasure. With their strength, teeth, and claws, it would be foolish to disregard them. Only once in the months that Christian lived at Sophistocat were we very frightened of him. He found a fur belt that had dropped off a coat, and delighted by this find, he ran down into the basement. We followed him to retrieve it. He was chewing the belt and making excited sucking sounds. We knew that this would be something he would be reluctant to give up. We tried to take it from him, but he flattened his ears and snarled a ferocious warning. He was an unrecognizable, wild animal. Undoubtedly, he would have attacked us if we had tried again to take the belt from him. We wanted to leave him, but we slowly moved a few yards away and talked to one another as if nothing had happened and as if we had forgotten about the belt. We realized we must not convey to him how frightened we were. It could have encouraged him to repeat this performance if he had sensed how effective it was. After about five minutes his excitement over the belt, and his anger, subsided. We spent the next few hours talking and playing with him very normally. We respected him for his distinct warning. This incident was never repeated, but we had been given an important reminder of Christian's potential danger.

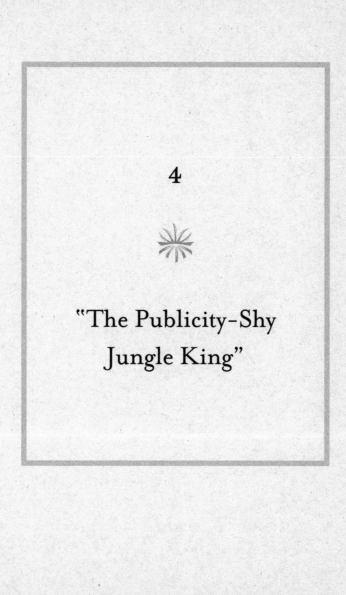

4

"The Publicity-Shy
Jungle King"

When the Lady Mayor of Kensington and Chelsea came into Sophistocat to meet Christian, she bent over to stroke him, and her elaborate chain of office dangled temptingly in front of him. He could not resist, and a large paw went out and swiped at it. The chain whirled around her neck. She was dazed but unhurt. Lions, monarchs by birth, are not impressed by the trappings of municipal office.

A diverse assortment of people met Christian, and some of them visited him regularly. One woman came into the shop with jelly-babies for the bear she heard lived there. She was greatly disappointed to hear that Christian was only a lion, and worse, was not tempted by the jelly-babies. Actresses Diana Rigg and Mia Farrow, customers at Sophistocat, loved meeting him, and came back to play with him. As Christian received considerable publicity, several people came into the shop concerned that we were just using him as a gimmick, but they were placated to see him so happy, healthy, and apparently very fond of us.

Having a lion became part of our lives, and we had to accept all the interest he aroused. If we were not with him we were continuously being asked about him. We had to listen patiently to people's stories about their "wild" cats, while others reminisced of their experiences in Africa. We were constantly asked, "How long is it before he becomes a man-eater?" It was impossible to relate such questions to

Christian, especially when watching him play with his best friend, Unity Bevis-Jones.

Unity met Christian in January 1970, one month after we had bought him. She heard that a lion lived at Sophistocat and rushed immediately to the shop. She visited Christian every afternoon, and her life revolved around him. She was so slight we were worried that he would unintentionally hurt her, but she handled him extremely well. She wore a thick coat and a rather mad felt hat for protection. This hat obscured most of her face, and it was only when Christian finally ate the hat several weeks later that we realized how attractive she was.

Unity was addicted to lions. One day in Rome, where she was an actress, she had decided that she wanted a lion, although she had not known any before. She managed to persuade the Rome Zoo to sell her a nine-month-old lioness that had just arrived at the zoo from Africa and had never been handled by humans before. It did not occur to Unity to be frightened of lions. After the lioness, called Lola, was delivered in a crate, she was surprised when her flatmate locked herself in her bedroom for a fortnight. Unity found landlords just as unreasonable, and she estimated that in the year and a half she and Lola lived together they moved about twenty times. When Unity had to return to England, Lola went to live with friends near Naples. Unity had an extraordinary affinity with Christian, and we could understand how she had managed to have a successful and accident-free relationship with Lola under much more difficult circumstances.

Each afternoon when Unity arrived at Sophisto-cat, Christian could be heard in the basement, noisily playing football with something, usually a plastic bucket. At the sound of her footsteps on the stairs, he would stop playing and listen and wait to see who it was. Unity would say: "Hello, Christian, it's me." Christian would grunt loudly, his normal greeting, and jump up at the locked door to peer at her through a small round hole. To prevent him from running upstairs when she opened the door,

Unity would ask Christian to move away before she came in. Although still close to the door, with a lionlike meow he would indicate that it was safe for her to come in. "No," she would say, "that's not far enough, go farther away." After a brief silence, Christian would grunt, and if the grunt sounded sufficiently distant to Unity's experienced ears, she then went into the basement and shut the door behind her. Christian would rush to greet her fondly and, grabbing her by the coat, would enthusiastically lead her around the basement.

If he was too boisterous, and ignored her when she said, "Don't be too rough," or "Stop it, Christian," she would edge toward the door when he was not looking and leave him. Christian would run to the door and meow and grunt. We would hear Unity say, "You're very naughty, and if you don't behave, I'm not coming in to play with you. I'm not a bucket, and I don't expect to be treated like one." As an apology, a few sorrowful grunts would follow, getting farther and farther from the door, to show

Unity she could come in without his rushing upstairs. Reprimanded, but always forgiven, he would now be gentle with her, and they would entertain each other with games and conversation for the rest of the afternoon.

One of Christian's most endearing characteristics was that he had individual relationships with all of us; only subtle differences, but different greetings, different games and tricks, and he knew exactly what each of us would let him get away with. Unity could never bring herself to refuse him anything. She often came to the garden with us, and the hours she spent with him each day in the basement made an enormous contribution to keeping him gentle. Animals have personalities that they can be encouraged to develop or express, and Unity taught us just how diverse Christian's personality was.

We gave more time and affection to Christian than either of us had consciously given to anything or anybody else before. It was a commitment and a responsibility that gave our lives a sense of purpose we had not previously felt. Our days were spent with him, and at night we put him in his room in the basement if we wanted to go out. One of us, quite often both of us at different hours, would let him out for a run around the shop late at night before going to bed. As the shop was closed on Sundays, and Christian enjoyed any change of environment, we sometimes took him on outings. But there are not many places you can take a lion in London. One day we took him to Kensington Gardens. He was frightened by all the space, and although on a long leash, he just hugged the fence for security. Not surprisingly, so many people gathered around him that it made this and similar outings to parks impossible.

We telephoned a Dr. Barnardo's Home to see if the children would enjoy a visit from Christian. The woman we spoke to was rather surprised, but when we assured her that he was not "dangerous," she accepted. We told her it was inadvisable for Christian to actually be with the children, and asked if there was an enclosed area for him. She suggested that the children could safely watch from inside the building, while "the lion grazes on the grass outside"!

But Christian's visit met with an unexpected lack of interest. Little faces were pressed against the windows for a few minutes, and then the children returned to their toys. While we had afternoon tea with the children, Christian was shut in a room. But a mischievous child let him out, and he came to look for us. The children screamed, scattered, and scrambled onto chairs and tables. Leaving chaos and probably many nightmares behind, we drove a confused little lion back to Sophistocat.

Christian was often invited with us to visit friends and other people, and occasionally we took him. On one visit Christian pushed open a bathroom door, and we ran when we heard a scream from our friend in the bath. It was difficult to know who was more frightened, Christian or our friend. The one household geared to incorporating a visit from a lion was that shared by Charles Bewick, Peter Bowen, and Margot the puma. We visited them quite often, and Christian spent Christmas Day there, while we visited friends in the country. Christian had been specifically not invited. Margot was a beautiful animal with an attractive purr, but her behavior was unpredictable, and it was difficult to relax in her company. She eventually ended up living on an estate in the country. We had hoped, rather naïvely, that Margot and Christian would be friends as we did not know any dogs strong enough to be his playmates. But Margot was a different species, a different sex, and a year older, and she was intensely antagonistic toward him. He was just indifferent. In fairness to her, Christian was an intruder on her territory. It was possible to have them in the same room together, but the only time he approached her, Margot whipped her paw at him and scratched his velvety nose. Christian did not care, but we were upset because he was to appear on television the next day!

In the middle of January 1970, a month after we had bought him, Thames Television heard that a lion was living at Sophistocat and invited Christian to appear on *Magpie,* their children's magazine pro-gram. He was only to appear for a few minutes, so we thought we could cope with it. We drove out to the television studios at Teddington, rather excited but uncertain as to how Christian would behave. Unfortunately, we had to have several rehearsals be-fore the live performance, and we felt this was rather unnecessary, as Christian reacted differently each time and was increasingly less cooperative. He was confused and dazzled by the glaring studio lights and frightened by the cameras when they advanced toward him. He was irritated at having to spend so much time on a leash, but long-suffering rather than angry. We regretted having accepted *Magpie*'s invitation, and nervously waited for the live per-formance. It was impossible to predict what Chris-tian would do. One of us was to be interviewed, and at the same time try to keep Christian in camera range. He was apparently a great success, although what appeared to be a playful romp on the studio floor was in reality a struggle to stop him from run-ning away.

Before his appearance on television, only a few newspapers had been interested in Christian. Suddenly he was more widely known, and there was much more curiosity about him, although the people who interviewed us seemed disappointed that owning a lion was less complicated than they had expected. The photographs they published were always of Christian yawning, with his teeth bared, and of course they appeared as vicious snarls. The publicity was good for Sophistocat, but we realized that if it was to continue we had to have control over the photographs published so that Christian could at least be portrayed accurately. We met a photographer, Derek Cattani, who got on well with Christian, and a pictorial record of his life in London began. The newspapers were quite welcome to buy a photograph if they wanted one.

People contacted us about wanting to use Christian in television commercials or for various promotional purposes. He was such an expense for us that we were prepared to be mildly commercial, providing he suffered no stress or discomfort. He liked outings and enjoyed his few sporadic "jobs," but in general he had a regular routine and a very stable life. He did a *Nights on the Wild Side* photo shoot for fashion magazine *Vanity Fair,* advertising night-gowns. It was easy work, for he was just required to lie on a bed with a beautiful model and be photo-graphed. The caption read:

> Beware the man-hunting feline! Some stalk their prey in the jungle; others play pussy at home in lounging lingerie that clings and ripples with the same cat-like grace. Our lingerie isn't meant for lonesome evenings—put it on when you're plan-ning to pounce, and if he doesn't, then get an-other cat for company!

Christian always enjoyed chewing hair, and the model had masses of it. He planned to pounce, and she became rather frightened and was actually heard to say: "My face is my fortune"! Restrained, Chris-tian bit a hole in the goat-skin bedspread and destroyed two satin pillows instead.

Several months later, the airline BOAC (now British Airways) contacted us. They were opening a new route to Africa and wanted Christian to make a very brief appearance at a promotional event where he created quite a sensation and easily outshone the other African representatives—potted palm trees and avocadoes. He earned thirty guineas, which we paid into his account at the bank. Photographs taken of Christian opening this account appeared in the bank house-journal with the caption "Tough Customer at Chelsea." It was an easy way of pacifying the manager about our overdrafts. We also did a series of Easter photographs for the newspapers, of Christian with six little chickens, and he was amazingly gentle and there were no casualties.

When he was about seven months old and obviously leaving his cub days behind, there was suddenly again a much greater and more widespread public interest. People were astounded that he was still so easy to manage. Experts from London Zoo and the Feline Advisory Bureau, for example, were astonished at how domesticated and well-behaved

Christian was. He was now regarded less as a novelty and more as a London personality owned "by two Australians." We were interviewed by several American and Australian newspapers and broadcasting services.

Jack de Manio, of the early-morning *Today* program on BBC Radio, telephoned to invite Christian to be interviewed. At our suggestion he came into Sophistocat to meet Christian beforehand, and we warned him that Christian could be very inarticulate if he was not in the mood, a disadvantage in a radio interview. As Christian had not yet roared, it was unlikely that Jack de Manio's listeners would be treated to his first attempt.

A car was sent to Sophistocat at 6:30 A.M. the next morning, and the three of us were taken to Broadcasting House. When we arrived the commissionaire blocked our entry to the building and, scarcely glancing at what was on the end of the leash, he challenged:

"No dogs allowed in here—it's the regulations."

"Do your regulations extend to lions?" we asked.

But people do not argue with lions, and as we strode past him into the building, he nimbly jumped aside.

Christian was far too interested in investigating the paraphernalia in the radio studio like tempting cords and wires, and looking at the faces pressed against the studio windows, to even consider making any lion-like noises in his interview. We spoke briefly on his behalf, but the caption in the following day's *Daily Mail* read:

MIKE-SHY CHRISTIAN FLOPS ON RADIO

We were mystified when we received a telephone call from the BBC at Sophistocat later in the day. Without being offered any explanation, we were curtly asked Christian's value, but it was not a question we had ever had reason to consider. Several days later, we read in Charles Greville's column in the *Daily Mail* what had happened. The caption was:

THE LION BEHIND BARS OF RED TAPE

BBC regulations stated that animals brought into the building had to be insured, but because of some slip-up, "an hilarious situation built up with poker-faced officialdom going about the business of taking out a policy against damage to their departed guests. And, presumably, damage to the hosts, although as events had already shown by that time, the animal could hardly raise a yawn in the studio, let alone breakfast off de Manio and his team . . . and the value of the publicity-shy jungle king? £500 say the owners.

Newspapers invariably rang us if a lion or other wild animal attacked or killed someone anywhere in the world. We enjoyed disappointing them with glowing reports of Christian's impeccable behavior. So many newspapers were inaccurate in their information about Christian that it was surprising we received only one hostile letter. After an article had appeared in an American newspaper in April 1970, a woman wrote a long abusive letter. She concluded:

"What do you intend doing with him when you tire of him? He must now be growing up and after the life you have forced him to lead, he must be getting vicious and dangerous. No doubt you have had his claws and perhaps even his teeth removed, so I'm sure no zoo would want him. End his miserable life and have him put to sleep." Declawing Christian had never been an option for us, and incorrect as she was about Christian's life with us at Sophistocat, we did share her concern for his future.

5

A Proposal

By April 1970, Christian was bored. He was then eight months old and rapidly outgrowing Sophistocat. Life had become repetitive and seemed to contain very few surprises for him. He was irritated that he had outgrown his favorite sitting spot on the stairs. It was too easy for him to climb all over the furniture in the shop, and now weighing 130 pounds, he was heavy enough to accidentally break the plate-glass windows. He was requiring more freedom, while we could only give him less. If he chose to behave badly, and he was now capable of inflicting serious damage, we knew we could not control him. Whereas he had previously been an attraction for the shop, his size was beginning to frighten customers away. George Lazenby, the actor of 007 James Bond fame, came to visit with a friend of ours one afternoon. Christian was sitting in the window, and even George could not be persuaded to enter the shop. So Christian was spending most of his time in the basement, and increasingly resenting any form of restriction.

He was less contented and so were we. It had become an enormous strain on us. We had a responsibility toward Christian, but also had to avoid creating any dangerous situations. It was inadvisable to wait and see what form his frustrations might take.

The question of his future, which had hung over us from the very beginning, now inescapably confronted us. We went to Longleat Safari Park again, for as we had discovered before we bought Christian, it seemed to offer the best living conditions for lions in England. This time we knew much more about lions. Because of the likelihood that Christian would soon be going there, we were proudly, but mistakenly, shown other sides of Longleat. We saw what an enormous commercial concern the Longleat-Chipperfield partnership had become, for apart from the lions in the Park, Mary Chipperfield provided an animal-hiring service for film and television companies. Also, some of the lions we saw were apparently part of a traveling circus. It was doubtful whether we could ensure that Christian would be introduced into a pride and live in the Park, and not be used for more obvious commercial purposes. We decided that for Christian, Longleat Safari Park was no longer a satisfactory solution.

To send him to a zoo would have been a betrayal of faith difficult for us to live with, but much more difficult for him. We now hoped to find someone with a large country estate who would love and care for him the same way that we did. Looking for other alternatives, we visited several private zoos. They were perhaps more rural than their city counterparts, but more amateurish, and just as restricting and insensitive.

One afternoon the actor Bill Travers came into the shop and was soon joined by his wife, actress Virginia McKenna. They had starred in the 1966 film *Born Free*, the story of Elsa the lioness who had been returned to the wild by Joy and George Adamson. The film, like the book, had been a huge hit, and although we were unfamiliar with either, we recognized the actors. We assumed that their association with lions had brought them to Sophistocat. Disappointingly, they were only shopping for a pine desk, but we were unable to resist the opportunity of introducing them to Christian. They were astonished to see a lion run toward us and greet us affectionately. We talked about Christian's life with us, and they understood our dilemma about his future. They were pleased we had "rescued" Christian from a cage at Harrods but disapproved of the purchasing and trafficking in exotic animals. Since starring in *Born Free* they had devoted their lives primarily to producing documentaries about animal conservation. Bill and Virginia had a much wider knowledge of lions than we had, and we asked them endless questions. We were flattered when they said they would like to come and see Christian again.

A few days later, Bill came into Sophistocat with James Hill, who was the director of the film *Born Free*. We wondered why James had come, and why he questioned us so extensively about Christian. We were surprised and delighted, then, when Bill invited us to dinner at his house at Leith Hill in Surrey. He said he would like to show us a documentary he had made about lions that had begun their lives in captivity.

Dinner with film stars. It seemed fitting that James Hill should collect us from Sophistocat in his Rolls-Royce, and to the astonishment of the World's Enders, we were grandly swept down to Surrey. After dinner we watched Bill's film *The Lions Are Free,*

showing what had since happened to the lions involved in the filming of *Born Free*. Twenty-four lions
had been used, yet, contrary to the theme of the
film, only after a long struggle by Joy, George, Bill,
and Virginia was George allowed to rehabilitate
three of them. None of the others would have the
chance to live a natural life. In *The Lions Are Free*, Bill
visited the three lions George had successfully rehabilitated, and although they had not seen him for
three years they remembered him, and he received
a fond greeting.

The film ended with Virginia visiting Whipsnade
Zoo to see Little Elsa, a lioness she had become
particularly fond of during the filming of *Born Free*.
Virginia called her name, and Little Elsa immediately recognized her and ran to the bars of the
compound. How could Virginia explain why they
could not greet each other as they always had? The
parallel with Christian was only too apparent, with
the probability that within weeks we would have to
condemn him to the same meaningless existence.

Sensing our feelings, Bill smiled and said: "I think we can help you solve the problem of Christian's future. We would like to arrange for him to be flown out to Africa where George Adamson can return him to the wild."

It was as if a prison sentence had suddenly, simply, been lifted. Of all the lions ever born in Europe, Christian had been offered an unprecedented reprieve. He was to go back where he belonged. Bill had contacted George Adamson in Kenya after his initial introduction to Christian at Sophistocat. George was extremely interested in the experiment of bringing a fifth-generation European lion for rehabilitation in Africa, and was confident it would be successful. Bill and James intended to make a documentary for television that would help to cover the considerable expenses involved.

We did not have to be converted to Bill and Virginia's proposal. We did worry, however, that because Christian had led such an unnatural life we may have delionized him to an extent that made rehabilitation impossible. George had assured Bill that Christian was still very young, and that it would take many more generations of lions existing in captivity before their natural instincts would be impaired. George intended to create a man-made pride of lions, incorporating Christian. We were to accompany Christian to Kenya and help him start to adjust to his new life. George would live with the lions and feed them until they had established their territory and were functioning effectively as a pride.

We realized it could not be assumed that Christian would have a long, natural life. On average lions live to eighteen to twenty years in zoos, but approximately nine to twelve years in the wild. Lions have to face territorial battles with one another, as well as droughts and scarcity of game, and only the strongest survive. When lions hunt animals as large as buffaloes, unless they kill efficiently, they can easily be injured or be killed themselves. And Christian, with his Chelsea background, would be starting with disadvantages. However, he would escape a long, safe, but totally pointless life in captivity, and would be given the opportunity to take his chance in his natural environment.

On our way back to London we spoke excitedly of the unpredictability of life. Where would Christian be now if someone else had bought him from Harrods? What would have happened if Bill and Virginia had not come into Sophistocat? By accident they walked into our problem of Christian's future and became involved in it. By buying Christian we had added new dimensions to our lives, and now unexpectedly to his. It would have been an unforgettable experience for us, but one that would be totally spoiled if Christian were to live the rest of his life in captivity. George Adamson now offered the perfect solution to our dilemma with Christian, a lion, it seemed, that had been marked for an extraordinary destiny. When we arrived back in London that night, Christian fittingly made his first attempt at a roar. It was immature but recognizable, and we were immensely proud.

6

The Lion at
World's End

B ill Travers flew to Kenya to assist in negotiations that had already begun with the Kenyan government. He was confident that this unusual project would be acceptable, but the plans became more complicated than had been anticipated. In principle, permission to make the documentary was not a problem. It would be good publicity for Kenya and help attract more tourists, still the main source of revenue. Even if the basic motivation was to maintain this industry, at the time there was an increasing awareness among most African governments of the need for the conservation and protection of animals. In the intervening years it has become obvious that even more urgent action is required, and there has been an alarming acceleration in the competition between man and wildlife for dwindling resources and habitats. The Kenyan government was also interested in having a record of George Adamson's methods of rehabilitating lions, and particularly the scientific documentation of such a unique experiment with a lion from England.

However, there had been considerable controversy in Kenya the previous year over the whole question of the rehabilitation of lions. A child had been slightly injured by one of George Adamson's lions, and this unfortunate incident provided an unfavorable background to our negotiations. Some members of the government viewed the rehabilitation of lions as a worthwhile project, but others felt that because of their earlier contact with humans, these lions would be likely to approach people in the game parks, and that could create a dangerous situation. Most people fear lions, and for Africans, they are a traditional natural enemy or competitor, so why bring yet another potential man-eater from England?

But the Kenyan government finally agreed to give their permission for Christian to come to Kenya if a suitable area could be found. It had to have water and game, and be in a region where there were neither tourists nor any immediate likelihood of a tourist area developing. It would have to be closed to hunting, and have no resident Africans or their cattle, which could be an easy temptation for the lions. Bill looked at several possibilities while he was in Kenya, but had to return to England, leaving George to continue the search.

Meanwhile, we had not heard from Bill and Virginia in several weeks. We did not dare telephone them in case we were told that it was no longer possible for Christian to go to Kenya. Finally, Bill rang and explained the delay, and he told us that George had just found two suitable areas, and it seemed likely that the Kenyan government would agree to the use of either.

Bill was confident enough to decide that filming would begin at Sophistocat the following Monday. The documentary, to be called *The Lion at World's End*, would be directed by James Hill, and it was to start with a reconstruction of Bill and Virginia's first meeting with Christian, then record the story exactly as it happened. The documentary would help to attract attention to the need for the protection and conservation of animals, and Christian, through extraordinary luck, was to be the subject and prime beneficiary of the film.

Our excitement was mixed with apprehension. After our experience at the television studios when Christian had appeared on the children's program, we realized that it was impossible to predict how he would react to being filmed. We did not know to what extent we would be involved in the filming, although having no acting ambitions we could reject the old theatrical axiom "Never compete with animals or children."

Bill and James gave strict instructions that Sophistocat was to remain unchanged for the filming. We were asked not to cut our hair, and to be as flamboyantly dressed and as "King's Road" as possible, instructions that we now rather regret. But as the shop would be closed to customers for one or two days, we thought it would be a nice gesture to the patient and tolerant owners if the shop appeared as smart as possible. On Sunday we repainted the walls and floor. It was a nicer gesture than we had intended, for it was an enormous shop and we worked hard all day. Christian was allowed upstairs only late in the afternoon, after the paint had dried on the floor. The last wall was still being completed when Christian knocked over the can, splashing paint everywhere. Surprised, he jumped back, but slipped and fell. Scrambling to his paws, he then ran to the other end of the shop. We were dismayed; white paw marks covered the black floor, and Christian, required to appear as a lion for the cameras the following morning, was an unrecognizable white animal. Until very late that night one of us was repainting the floor, while in the basement, the other, armed with towels and turpentine, was struggling to clean Christian, who just thought it was a new game.

Next day Sophistocat was transformed into a film set. At first Christian was dazzled by the bright lights and confused by all the unfamiliar equipment and camera crew. But this helped to keep him unusually subdued, and he only scattered the crew a few times. Bill and James were familiar with filming animals, and were very patient and undemanding. Christian, bored with the normal shop routine, enjoyed the day and was so cooperative that Bill described him as a "one-take lion." We were to participate fully in the filming, and could forget about the cameras by concentrating rather intensely on Christian, who performed magnificently. Unfortunately, our few lines of dialogue were later dubbed in excruciatingly broad Australian accents, as our voices sounded "too English."

The following day we filmed at the Moravian Close, but Christian resented sharing his garden with so many other people and was very unco-operative. This was probably because of his strong territorial claim, and although he loved chasing soccer balls, that day he totally ignored them. Bill and James wanted to film some slow-motion sequences, but when we finally succeeded in getting Christian to run or move, he stopped as soon as he heard the noisy slow-motion camera. Eventually, with no other alternative, we broke all our rules by encouraging him to chase us. We were irresistible and Christian could not believe his luck. Despite our torn clothing, the result was an enjoyable and worthwhile day's filming.

Several days later we saw the rushes of the first two days of filming. Christian looked beautiful, the slow-motion sequences of him running and play-ing were stunning, and none of us, not even Bill or Virginia, had seen a lion in slow motion before. For the first time we really appreciated his strength, power, and perfect coordination.

This might have been Christian's last visit to the garden, because the Moravian minister, although extremely fond of him, had reluctantly told us that he could no longer exercise there. Like most other people, he had been very tolerant, but other people had access to the garden and could not now be ex-pected to cope with Christian's boisterousness as we could. The day he had obstinately refused to get off the roof of the minister's car might also have been an influencing factor. But when we told him that we expected to be in Kenya in a few weeks' time, he kindly compromised by allowing us to come to the garden at 6:30 A.M. Our lives had to be considera-bly readjusted, and Christian was now finding his life at Sophistocat increasingly monotonous and frustrating. He needed his day to be broken by an afternoon outing, so the early-morning exercise did not suit him either. Bill suggested building a compound for Christian in the garden at their house at Leith Hill near Dorking in Surrey, so that the three of us could live there until we left for Kenya.

When the compound was completed, Christian left the King's Road and London forever. Many of his World's End friends gathered to say good-bye. After living for several weeks fearing an accident, it was a relief to leave only pleasant memories behind. But we were also sad; our five very happy, unrepeatable months with Christian in London were over.

7

Country Life

Bill and Virginia's house at Leith Hill was surrounded by an attractive, rambling garden. Although only thirty miles from London, it overlooked a valley of unspoiled countryside. When we arrived, their children and dogs were safely inside the house, and Christian had a taste of the freedom that awaited him in Africa. For the first time in his life he could do exactly what he wanted to do. He ran around the lawns, occasionally sniffing daffodils, and into the woods through the bluebells. It was a beautiful but incongruous setting for a lion. He continually came back to us to show how happy he was.

It was necessary that Christian should live in the compound, but luckily he seemed very pleased with it. It measured twenty-five yards by fifteen, and it enclosed a huge tree, several shrubs, and a colorful gypsy caravan. He was so excited that his first reaction was to climb the tree, but as he had never climbed one before, he was confused as to how to turn around and get down again. He just waited for us to help him. Bill thought that Christian would sleep under a shrub, but we suspected he would prefer to sleep in the caravan. We were to live in another caravan beside the compound. It was summer and the sun was shining, and it was so peaceful in comparison with London.

That first night we sold Christian. A contract had been drawn up between us and the film company making *The Lion at World's End*. The whole project would be an expensive one, and while it was unlikely we would not fully cooperate, we were required to relinquish to the company our ownership of Christian. We surrendered all legal control over Christian's future. We were paid five hundred pounds, and we tried to view the transaction as a necessary formality in his best interests. But we felt guilty, and preferred to think of Christian becoming a Kenyan citizen rather than the mere property of a film company.

Christian slept in the caravan, of course. He greeted us effusively the next morning, relieved that we had not abandoned him and returned to London during the night. He seemed untroubled by his change of surroundings and oblivious to the fact that we no longer technically owned him.

We expected to be at Leith Hill only a few weeks, but George was still having difficulty in finding an area that both he and the Kenyan government found suitable, as the two he had originally proposed had not been approved. We were anxious to get Christian to Kenya, but we dreaded to think how unattractive and desolate the district that finally met all the requirements might be. Always expecting to leave shortly, we waited while George continued searching, and the weeks passed. Fortunately it was summer and the weather was usually pleasant. We spent restful days reading, sunbathing, playing with Christian, and friends came down to visit. But as we were both basically city-oriented, one of us would occasionally go to London for a few days.

Unexpectedly, Leith Hill became an important phase in Christian's life. He had fewer restrictions, a less complicated life, and a more clearly defined territory to live in. For the first time, he experienced the natural cycle of a day. Sleeping in the caravan was a hangover from his life as a London lion. It was often hot, and he was lethargic during the day, but he became rather boisterous in the late afternoons and evenings. After living at Sophistocat with Christian for five months, and regularly putting him to

Below: Virginia McKenna, Bill Travers, Ace, and John in Christian's gypsy caravan at Leith Hill.

Above: Christian at Leith Hill, aged ten months. His mane had begun to grow.

Bottom: Christian playing wheelbarrows with his best friend, Unity Bevis-Jones.

Right: John playing with Christian at Leith Hill.

Below: John removing a twig from Christian's mouth at Leith Hill.

Bottom: John, Christian, and Ace relaxing at Leith Hill.

Left: Ace and John checking on Christian in his crate at Heathrow Airport.

Bottom: Loading Christian's crate onto the East African Airways flight to Nairobi.

George Adamson, Bill Travers, Ace, and John with Christian at Nairobi Airport.

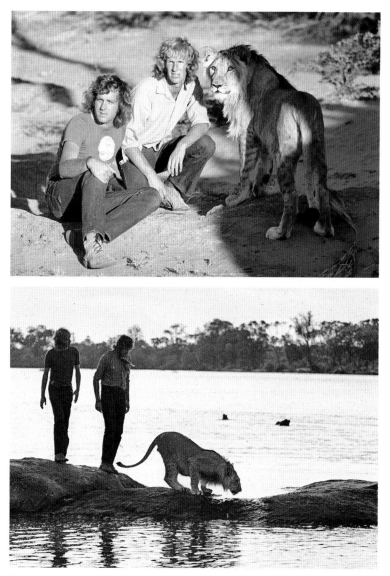

Top: John, Ace, and Christian at Kora.

Bottom: Christian investigates the Tana River while John and Ace watch for crocodiles.

The first camp beside the Tana River.

Three-month-old Katania with Boy, who had starred in the film *Born Free*.

George Adamson and Christian at Kora.

Christian meets Katania for the first time.

Christian preferred to leap from rock to rock in the Tana River, rather than get wet.

Christian picking his way carefully through the thick thorn bushes at Kora.

bed at about 8:30 P.M., we now appreciated that lions are naturally nocturnal. We spent most of our time in the compound, as he would look discontented if we were not with him. Yet he often ignored us once we were inside, for even if he did not want to play with us, as part of his "pride," he just enjoyed the companionship. A double-gate system made entries and exits from the compound easy and safe.

Bill and Virginia had three young children and several dogs, and from his compound Christian watched their movements closely. He would have loved to be included in their games. At Sophistocat, if Christian had to be in the basement, he was unaware of what he was missing upstairs. Christian did not like to be left out of anything and expected to have the freedom to decide if he wanted to participate. At Leith Hill a twelve-foot-high wire fence prevented him from joining in, but not from seeing the tempting games from which he was excluded. Unless we were with him, he paced the fence with frustration, and very quickly wore a path along it.

By now it might have been a cage he was pacing in the same pointless way. After the initial mutual curiosity between Christian and the dogs, they quickly lost interest in one another. But if one of the dogs strayed too close to the fence, Christian would tensely crouch and flatten his ears, imagining he was invisible, but he forgot about his tail, which swished in excitement. Then he would charge the fence and succeed in frightening away the dog, and because of the number of times he succeeded in stalking and almost knocking us to the ground, we felt his natural instincts had not been impaired.

We decided to begin Christian's preparation for Africa in a small way at Leith Hill. By comparisons we had made with other lions at Longleat Safari Park or at zoos, Christian was big for his age, but he needed to be as strong as possible for his new life. With constant exercise and this outdoor life, he looked even healthier and continued to grow rapidly, his body now more in proportion with his head and paws. On a rope from his tree we hung a sack filled with straw, and he adored attacking it, often swinging entirely off the ground. This was good practice for Kenya, and helped to develop his muscles. He had learned to keep his claws sheathed when we were playing with him; sharp, inch-long claws are an important weapon for a lion, and attacking the sack strengthened them and taught him how to use them efficiently. We also changed Christian's diet. Lions in the wild usually kill in the evenings and have a varied diet. Christian was now given a small milk and Farex meal in the morning and one large evening meal. In addition to raw meat, he had dried meat, carrots, and cow's liver, and sometimes we gave him the head or stomach of a cow. His presence at Leith Hill had not been publicized, and the local butcher, mystified by our meat orders, asked, "What on earth are you two feeding, a crocodile?" As he knew we were living with Bill and Virginia, a lion would have been a far more reasonable assumption.

His new diet improved his coat. It became thicker

and softer, and was a beautiful lion-caramel color. His partially black mane became more pronounced, and he was growing into an extremely handsome lion. He spent more time cleaning and grooming himself, although he was never as fastidious as most domestic cats. His tongue was so rough that his licks on our faces could almost draw blood. He had lost his milk teeth, and he initiated his new ones by destroying several rungs of the ladder to his caravan.

He also had more scope to express himself at Leith Hill, and because we had more time to spend with him and appreciate him away from the demands of the city, our relationship with him grew even deeper and more affectionate. Unity came down from London several times each week to spend the day with him, and new games were invented. He particularly enjoyed playing "wheelbarrows" with her and became adept at tapping ankles and tripping people. He had a variety of toys, a new tire, and several shrubs to play lions behind. He was content, and we found him irresistibly entertaining. Considering his size, he played extremely gently with us and remained easy to manage. It was perfectly safe for any of our visitors to come into the compound with him, except for children who could accidentally be knocked over. A lion prepared to play "wheelbarrows" must have, in addition to a sense of humor, a love for the human race.

Sometimes when it rained he grew quite wild, and then we stayed outside the compound. There was a difficult period when he became aware that he could easily prevent us from leaving the compound by jumping up and holding us with his large front paws. Our smacks just made him more determined. Smacking a lion in a situation such as this required considerable audacity. But within a few days he realized that behavior like this was self-defeating, for it meant we spent less time with him. He decided it was best to continue to cooperate.

We had bought Christian when he was very young, and it had taken months for us to build up our relationship with him. We admired the courage Bill and Virginia had shown playing their roles in the film *Born Free* and working with a cast of many adult lions. There was less opportunity for them to develop relationships that were similar to ours with Christian. As we were soon to leave for Africa, it was pointless for him and Virginia to become too friendly with Christian, but they often came down to his compound to see him. When they were with him, because of their experience with lions, they handled him well.

Christian's life at Leith Hill continued to be filmed, with particular emphasis on the beginnings of his rehabilitation. He had a strong fascination for the documentary director James Hill, and most of our time was spent preventing Christian from jumping on him. James insisted that he was not frightened but just did not want "to have my new trousers torn." He seemed to have new trousers on each day we filmed, and he directed more comfortably from outside the compound.

Bill decided to film Christian's first visit to an

English beach. We were not enthusiastic; 3 A.M. is an unappealing time to begin a day, and we knew that it would be us Christian would trample on during the sixty miles there and back. He was now too big to travel in a car, so we went in Bill and Virginia's Dormobile, a motorized caravan. It was the first English beach we had seen as well, and it was gray, dismal, and deserted. But there was a beautiful dawn, and we filmed several sequences of Christian and the four of us running along the beach. He had no intention of getting wet. He enjoyed the outing, but finally tired of waiting on the leash each time until the cameras were positioned. It was unwise to irritate a lion of his size, so we took him home. His paw marks must have confused bathers later in the day.

Christian had now been at Leith Hill for ten weeks, and his life there was losing its attraction. And for us, too, our caravan seemed to shrink in size daily. There had been days of incessant rain, and we found the continuing delays depressing.

Christian was becoming frustrated again, and the strain we had felt during his last weeks at Sophisto-cat returned. He occasionally climbed the wire of his compound. We hoped that this was just a way of attracting our attention rather than an attempt to escape, but we added an overhang for security.

On August 12, 1970, Christian celebrated his first birthday. Unity made him a birthday cake of minced meat. It had one candle on top, and before Christian ate it and the cake, we made a wish that he would soon be in Kenya.

8

Christian's Parents

We had to prepare Christian for his journey to Kenya, as the long flight to Nairobi would be an ordeal. He was to fly with East African Airways, and regulations required him to travel by crate in the pressurized hold. It was an eleven-hour flight, but because Christian would be put in his crate at Leith Hill, he faced at least fifteen hours of confinement. When Bill was making arrangements with the airline company, a representative said:

"There seems to be a mistake, Mr. Travers. Surely you don't intend flying a lion from England to Africa—that's just taking coals to Newcastle."

We investigated the whole question of Christian's flight very thoroughly, and telephoned several animal dealers and zoos for information about the best methods of safely transporting animals. Our research revealed that there was no agreement or even any particular interest in the transportation of exotic animals. We would like to believe that today animal transportation is a much more sensitive and sophisticated operation, but while great care is taken with some animals, most livestock are still transported around the world with little regard for their well-being. There is, for example, ongoing criticism of the conditions under which Australian sheep are shipped to the Middle East. Some of the people we spoke to suggested a small crate to make it impossible for the animal to turn around; the less room, the less scope the animal would have to move and injure himself. We spoke to Oliver Graham-Jones, who had been senior vet at the London Zoo, and was well known at the time for the publicized attempts at insemination of Chi-Chi the panda, who had to be transported from London to Moscow and back. He advised that Christian should be mildly tranquilized by adding a sedative to his food, and that this would safely minimize any frustration. Christian would probably sleep for most of the journey. We decided to order a crate large enough for him to sit upright and turn around in, with bars on one end and a sliding panel at the other. We specifically requested that there be no rough surfaces or sharp edges on which he could injure himself.

When the crate was delivered, we put it in his compound for Christian to become familiar with it. He was fed in it, and we shut his caravan at night to encourage him to sleep in it. Each day we shut him in for short periods so that the actual journey would be less of a shock.

East African Airways quoted a charge at the time of £2 per pound for flying Christian to Kenya, so we had to weigh him. We borrowed some scales from the even more mystified butcher and tied them to a rope hanging from a tree. We put an empty sack under Christian's stomach, lifted him up, and slipped both ends of the sack onto the hook at the bottom of the scales. He dangled helplessly but good-naturedly. It had been an effort for Bill and us to lift him, and we were not surprised when we saw that he weighed 160 pounds. A veterinary certificate of health was also required, and Christian was examined by a vet and inoculated with Catovac to protect him from diseases he would have no immunity against in Africa.

We had always wanted to see Christian's parents at Ilfracombe Zoo in Devon, and because of the long delay at Leith Hill, we now had the opportunity to visit them. The zoo was typical of the many small country zoos scattered around England at the time, most of which have since closed. Because Ilfracombe is a popular holiday resort, there were accommodation chalets attached to the zoo. There was a rather tacky fairground atmosphere, and depressingly small and basic cages for an assortment of chimpanzees, llamas, birds, and even a few scruffy kangaroos. The lions were the star attraction, and Christian's parents, Butch and Mary, were the most magnificent lions we had ever seen. Despite their restricted living conditions, they looked very healthy. Unlike lions in the wild, which rest between kills until hungry again, Butch and Mary were fed daily so that they did not roar at night and disturb the vacationers in the nearby chalets. Christian looked very like his handsome, heavily maned, three-year-old father. They were an affectionate couple, but they incessantly paced the cement floor of their small cage. The owner of the zoo was prepared to sell them for £500, but we did not dare ask Bill if Butch and Mary could come to Kenya, too.

We asked the owner about Christian's sisters, and he told us the name of the animal dealer to whom he had sold them. We contacted this dealer, but as he had sold fifty-eight lion cubs in 1969 and kept no detailed records, he could only say that they had been sold to a circus. Christian's sister at Harrods, who had been called Marta, had been purchased with a fraudulent check, and immediately resold to an undisclosed person. The following letter sent to the Harrod's buyer Roy Hazle provided some explanation:

December 26, 1969
H.M. Prison
Jobb Avenue
Brixton
London SW 2

Dear Sir,

I have been told that you and the lady that works with you have been worried about the lion cub I got from you. May I put your mind at rest and tell you that it is now in a very nice home where it has a very nice shed which is heated and a big garden to play in. Two nice girls are looking after it as it is the family pet and it gets the best of food to live on. It has a dozen eggs and fresh milk every day and plenty of meat, it's in the home of a film star. So please don't worry about it and tell the lady who used to look after it that it could not get a better home. This will give her a little comfort because I know she liked her very much. So please don't worry it's being well looked after.

Yours sincerely

J. R. Styles

Despite this letter and further efforts to locate Marta, no trace of her was ever found.

Ironically, many dogs and cats have pedigrees, yet then it was almost impossible to trace a lion's history as so few records were kept. Major national zoos now protect gene pools and keep precise records of individual animals. Butch had been purchased from the Rotterdam Zoo and may have been related to Elsa, because Joy and George Adamson had sent Elsa's sisters to the Rotterdam Zoo from Kenya in 1956. Christian's family history was depressingly typical of animals in captivity, and by buying Christian we had unwittingly participated in this trade.

Inevitably we compared Christian's future with the life of his parents—freedom, instead of cement, bars, and boredom. Neither of us had visited a zoo where we believed that animals were both successfully and happily confined. Zoos should be constantly monitored, and certain standards maintained. We feel that being anti-zoo is unrealistic and that zoos today are doing invaluable scientific and genetic research, which will ensure the conservation of endangered species. Zoos have had to reinvent themselves and today are under intense scrutiny. Species such as the Arabian oryx, the white rhinoceros in South Africa, and the black rhinoceros in Kenya and Tanzania, which are almost extinct in their natural habitat, have been saved. Christian had awakened in us a general feeling of responsibility toward all other animals. Bill and Virginia both said that their association with the lions during the filming of *Born Free* had had an enormous influence on their lives, and we frequently discussed with them the whole question of the conservation and protection of wild animals. We realized for the first time how drastically short-sighted man has been. Many of these issues have since become even more urgent, with the competition between man and wildlife for habitats and resources, including water, the degradation of the environment, and the ramifications of climate change. What has become even more obvious to us is the interrelationship between man and the natural environment, and how holistic any solutions will have to be.

Sitting in our caravan at Leith Hill, we decided to create the best zoo in the world. Our zoo would be an example to all others, provide the best possible living conditions in captivity, and make accessible the most up-to-date information about animal life. World experts would work in conjunction with leading architects and designers to create an environment of the most sensitive and sophisticated nature. In addition to our perfectly exhibited, healthier, and happier animals, we would provide lecture halls where zoologists and other specialists lectured, and cinemas to show wildlife documentaries about animals in their natural state. We would have bookshops, and a library of books and films. Our zoo would become a center of research and information, providing standards and advice on the conservation and care of animals in captivity, for people all over the world.

We began to think how we could have designed a more sympathetic compound for Christian that would have resulted in his feeling less restricted. Why do so many animals in zoos have to live in compounds and cages that have such monotonous symmetry, no variety, practical but cold cement floors, and no evidence of any imagination in their design? Why not have compounds where humans walk through an enclosed corridor into the center and where the animals have the freedom to walk almost entirely around the humans? There would be at least some transference of the feeling of restriction. Looking back, we are happy to note that some of these ideas have been incorporated into the redesigning and building of some enclosures, and the animals' well-being has become a priority. Frankfurt Zoo in Germany has been a leader in this field, and at Taronga Conservation Society Australia, some imaginative enclosures have been designed.

We waited for so long at Leith Hill that Christian outgrew his crate. We noticed that when he was shut in, he sometimes frustratedly pawed the vertical bars and rubbed his pads quite raw. For his next-larger crate, we requested that the bars be placed horizontally, which would make it impossible for him to injure himself in this way. Although the company that made the crate had been supplying zoos and animal dealers for many years, they had never been asked to make this very obvious improvement. This seemed indicative of just how insensitive animal traders were.

After three months at Leith Hill, we were beginning to despair that George would ever find a suitable site for Christian's rehabilitation, and we dreaded any alternative we might be forced to consider. We were depressed by the ongoing delay and the cramped living conditions. By now we were less starstruck, and we questioned how we were being portrayed in the film. We feared Christian was becoming just another animal in another Bill Travers and Virginia McKenna wildlife documentary. But Christian's story was unique. He was the undoubted star of the film, and we were all bit players. As in London, when the situation with Christian seemed to be approaching breaking point, the next stage in his life emerged just in time. A cable arrived from George Adamson. Christian would be leaving England for Kenya in a few days.

9

"Coals to Newcastle"

At 3:30 P.M. on August 22, 1970, Christian was led into his crate, not for the customary few minutes, but for at least fifteen hours. Pouring rain was to be his last memory of England. He was fed mild tranquilizers in pieces of meat, and then we carried his crate to the van that was to take him to London's Heathrow Airport. Lions have no luggage, and we could leave his leash behind as there would be no further use for it. Unity had of course come to Leith Hill to say good-bye to him and tear-fully promised to visit him in Kenya.

Following Bill and Virginia in their car, we traveled to the airport in the van with Christian, who was confused but not alarmed. The car with our cameraman was stopped by the police for film-ing without a permit, for cutting across traffic, and causing an obstruction. But the combination of Virginia McKenna and a lion on his way to Africa persuaded the surprised policeman to be lenient, and the convoy was allowed to proceed. At Heath-row we drove straight out onto the tarmac and parked beside the East African Airways plane. Bur-lap was tied around the crate as insulation against the cold on the long night flight. The tranquilizers were proving effective, for Christian was quite re-laxed, despite the noise from other aircraft and the curious crowd that had gathered. At 5:30 P.M., Christian's crate was forklifted into the small pres-surized hold of the plane. It was a dramatic and worrying moment when we all realized there was a possibility that in the hold, alone among the luggage, Christian could die.

We left England at 7:00 P.M. with Bill and the film crew, and with Christian somewhere underneath us. The only scheduled stop, before Jomo Kenyatta Airport in Kenya, was in Paris one hour later. We were allowed to climb into the hold, where to our great relief we found Christian sleepy and calm. We decided that it was unnecessary to give him more tranquilizers, so we just slipped pieces of meat through the bars to him and refilled his water bowl. But the most demanding and longest part of the flight still lay ahead.

We landed in Nairobi at 7:00 A.M. Uninterrupted sunshine is assumed in Africa, as it is in Australia or Los Angeles, but it was overcast and cold. While we had checked that it was not the rainy season, we had overlooked that it would be winter. On the tarmac we anxiously waited for Christian's crate to be unloaded. He had survived! His ordeal was nearly over, but no longer tranquilized, he was very agitated. George Adamson was there to meet us, and he arranged for Christian to be wheeled off to an animal-holding compound, where he waited while we went through Immigration and Customs. Christian was relieved to be let out of his crate, and greeted us affectionately. George described him as "a handsome, friendly little fellow." Though he was uninjured and unmarked, Christian walked unsteadily and looked totally exhausted. His eyes were bleary, his coat had lost condition, and he seemed thinner. We could just not believe that after all the delays and frustrations Christian was safely in Kenya, and had escaped the fate of a life of captivity in the United Kingdom.

At last we had met George Adamson, who had first rehabilitated Elsa and knew more about lions than anyone else in the world, and who was to introduce Christian into the wild. He was a surprisingly small and dapper figure wearing a stiffly laundered safari suit, and he had neatly trimmed gray hair and a pointed goatee beard. He was soft-spoken but had piercing blue eyes that seemed to examine us, and in his Foreword he says he immediately had confidence in Christian but was not so sure about us! Only after a few days did he relax in our company. He was intelligent and amusing and admitted to his excitement and enthusiasm for the challenge of rehabilitating Christian.

The area allotted by the Kenyan government for this purpose was at Kora, near Garissa, two hundred and eighty miles northeast of Nairobi. To reach Kora, a final track of twenty miles had been cleared through the bush by George's brother, Terence Adamson, with an African labor force. Bill and George decided to make the journey in two stages in order to provide sufficient time for the camp to be prepared for our arrival. It would also be easier for Christian.

Kora had been offered because no one else wanted it. George described it as a desolate, unattractive part of Kenya. Few Africans live there, there were disease-carrying tsetse flies, and in the wet season it could be inaccessible. The game, while not abundant, would be adequate for Christian and the other lions in the pride that George intended to form. For the exclusive use of this unwanted land the film company had to pay £750 a year.

Christian remained in the holding compound at the airport for two days. We stayed in Nairobi, and several times each day drove out to see and feed him. He was apparently content to sleep if we were not there, but the flight seemed to have exhausted and disoriented him. Our visits attracted enormous crowds of Africans, and we realized that most of them had never seen a lion or many other indigenous animals. Until the early 1970s, only tourists could afford to visit the game parks. Each time Christian walked toward the gate of the compound, the crowd stepped back apprehensively. As we talked to various officials at the airport, it was apparent that they did not see the point of trying to rehabilitate a lion, let alone flying one from England at such expense.

We visited Nairobi National Park and saw many

animals in their natural environment, yet we were only fifteen miles from Nairobi and the Hilton Hotel was clearly visible on the horizon. Bill had the opportunity to show George and several other people the rough-cut of the English sequences in the film, and George was particularly interested to see a lion filmed in slow motion for the first time.

Within two days Christian had fully recovered from his flight, so early next morning we left Nairobi in several Land Rovers for the first stage of the journey. Christian traveled in the back of George's Land Rover, and to our concern, he paced relentlessly and quickly rubbed bare patches on his nose and forehead from the wire barrier between him and the front seats. We stopped frequently to give him water and to try to pacify him, and George probably thought that we were unnecessarily worried about our pampered lion. On one of these breaks George warned us that Christian could run off if we let him out of the vehicle, and we were very proud when much to George's surprise he obediently jumped back in.

As the day progressed it became increasingly hot, dry, and desolate. We had been depressed by George's description of Kora, and now we could see for ourselves the nature of the country that Christian was to live in. We drove two hundred miles, and just before nightfall arrived at a temporary camp, where we were to spend two nights, prepared by the safari company engaged to look after us. Christian was exhausted, and we led him into a small compound that had been built for him. We decided to put our beds in with him, and he promptly climbed onto one of them and fell asleep. His first night in the African bush!

In the stillness and refreshing coolness of the African evening, we sat down to a superbly set table where Africans in flowing blue kaftans and red boleros and caps served us a delicious three-course meal. It was a surreal but pleasant surprise. At dinner George relaxed and asked us to call him "George," and he told us about the other lions that were to be rehabilitated with Christian. For his man-made pride George already had two other lions waiting at Naivasha, and in a few days he would have to return to collect them. One was Katania, a four-month-old lioness, who had been found and given to George, her mother being presumed dead. The other was Boy, a seven-year-old lion who had led an extraordinary life.

In 1963, when they were young cubs, Boy and his sister, Girl, were abandoned or lost and were found by Colour Sgt. Ryves of the Scots Guard Regiment based near Nairobi. They were lovingly raised by his wife, Hildegarde, and their two young daughters, Jenny and Patricia. The cubs were so friendly and popular that they became the regimental mascots. When the regiment returned to the U.K., there was even a suggestion that Boy and Girl would go with them, but luckily they were given to Joy and George Adamson for rehabilitation. Before being returned to the wild, the cubs were to be used in the film *Born Free*, and Girl played Elsa. Most of the other lions used in the filming were sold to zoos and circuses, which angered Joy, George, Bill, and Virginia, and created controversy. In April 1965, Boy and Girl moved with George to Meru National Park.

Their rehabilitation had been successful, but in October 1969 Joy had quite by chance found Boy emaciated and badly injured, perhaps by a buffalo. He was operated on by the experienced wildlife vets Dr. Tony Harthoorn and his wife, Sue, and during the complicated operation they inserted a steel pin into one of Boy's legs. Joy and George nursed him for nine months at Naivasha, where Joy lived. It was a fortunate coincidence that Bill had contacted George about Christian at the time when Boy was almost well enough to be released again. George would leave our camp in a few days to collect Boy and Katania from Naivasha.

Next morning Christian had his first walk in Africa. We symbolically took off his collar, now permanently discarded, and followed him with Bill and George. The country was barren, with many thornbushes, and totally featureless, and Christian, who had appeared so big in a London furniture shop, was dwarfed by his surroundings. It was extremely hot, and he just walked quietly, absorbing everything. Instinctively, he knew how to remove thorns from his tender paws with his teeth, and we saw that the color of his coat was a natural camouflage. He was so obviously in his rightful environment.

Since it was a waterless region, it was unlikely that we would see any other animals. But late that afternoon a stray gombi, a large domestic African cow, came wandering toward the camp. Separated from its herd, it was looking for water or food. Christian saw the gombi and immediately began to stalk it. The animal had enormous sharp horns, and George warned us to stop Christian, for as he was so inexperienced he could easily be injured. He would not be restrained, so George raced to his Land Rover and drove between Christian and the gombi, which then ran off. Before Christian could follow it, we both grabbed him to put him in the Land Rover. For the second time in his life he snarled a terrifying warning and flattened his ears, and we instantly re-leased him. The gombi had disappeared, and Christian, justifiably angry, reluctantly followed us back to camp.

George was impressed by Christian's perfect, instinctive stalking of the gombi, and explained to us how he had fanned out in a wide semicircle, using the natural cover of the bushes. He had been correctly positioned so that the wind would not carry his scent to the gombi and alert it. George said, "We won't have any trouble adapting young Christian to the wild," and we were very proud.

It was now eighty miles to our final camp at Kora. But the road was rough and covered with powdery volcanic dust. We had to drive very slowly. As we drew closer to the camp on the Tana River, to our relief the countryside became slightly more fertile and varied. Among other animals we saw elephants, waterbucks, and some giraffes, and Africa began to come alive for us. We drove past a village whose inhabitants were wearing simple cloth wraps, necklaces, and bracelets. They were the first Africans we had seen apparently living as they had for centuries and not wearing drab Western clothes.

For the last twenty miles it was often necessary to use the four-wheel drive on the Land Rovers, particularly when crossing sandy riverbeds, and it was obvious why the area was sometimes inaccessible in the wet season. We arrived late in the afternoon to find the camp in an unexpectedly beautiful setting. Our tents were among the distinctive Doum palms, beside the wide Tana River. Christian's long journey was over, and we could not believe we had actually got him to where he was to live. No doubt many challenges lay ahead, like meeting the other lions and just surviving.

George left the next morning to collect the other lions from Naivasha, and was away for several days. We were thoroughly spoiled; our tents were comfortable and insect-free, our meals were provided, hot showers were prepared, and our clothes were washed and somehow even ironed. Christian had a compound near the tents to sleep in at night. The Africans with the safari company were terrified of him, however, and if he teased them too often we had to keep him in the compound during the day, as well. Because of the heat, we were all lethargic. Christian behaved like the worst tourist, avoiding the sun and lolling on our camp beds at every opportunity, probably dreaming of cooler weather in England.

In the early mornings before it became too hot, or in the late afternoons, we went for walks with Christian. We will never forget the freedom of just walking with him after the eight months in England so full of our imposed restrictions. He would bossily push his way in front of us and always insist on leading. But he was easy to direct and showed no inclination to wander off by himself. Fortunately, on these walks we did not meet any other animals, for we knew we would not be able to restrain him. If we went swimming, he sat in the shade and watched. He was fascinated by the baboons barking at him from across the river, and he observed the hippo-potami that occasionally surfaced and the croco-diles that ominously slid into the water whenever we appeared.

Filming continued intermittently, and to every-one's surprise the "King's Road Australians" adapted very easily to Africa compared to the English film crew. We were used to the heat and did not get sun-burned, drove the vehicles and had a good sense of direction, loved the bush, swam in the river, and of course, had confidence and ease with lions.

In several ways Christian seemed very much a be-ginner with a lot to learn. With his big paws he was rather clumsy and inept at climbing rocks, and we often had to show him the way or help him. For the first time in his life he was not wholly dependent on us for amusement, but we were slightly concerned by his lack of interest in investigating anything by him-self. There were many thornbushes, and although he was able to pull the thorns out of the pads of his paws, he often just looked helpless and waited for us to do it. His pads were still soft, and because of the long walks and the thorns they became quite raw, but they quickly began to toughen.

He was content and free and very gentle with us. Although now a large animal, he would still sometimes spontaneously leap into our arms, a gesture of affection that could now almost knock us to the ground. Soon other lions would arrive to hopefully make his life more complete.

10

A Lion's Lion

While George went to Naivasha to collect Boy and Katania, and we stayed by the river, Terence Adamson was building a permanent camp for George in much less attractive surroundings, several miles from the Tana River. This was to discourage the lions from swimming across the crocodile-infested river to the other side, which was a hunting block, where hunters pay for a license to hunt specific animals and where there was a real danger that the lions could be shot. George intended to live at Kora for at least two years, which would give him time to form a pride, and the lions would have the chance to establish their territory and operate independently. This second camp had several huts and tents within two large wire compounds.

A few days later George returned with Boy and Katania, and they were taken to his camp. In two days they had both recovered from their long journey, and it was time for Christian to be introduced to his first lions. The initial test in his rehabilitation was that he should be able to assimilate into a life with other lions and show that he had not been disadvantaged by his life among humans. George explained that the introduction would have to be a gradual one, spread perhaps over weeks or months. He wanted to live with Christian in one compound, separated by a strong, high wire fence from Boy and Katania in the other compound. Living side by side, they would develop a familiarity, and eventually could be fully introduced. As in all relationships, human or animal, compatibility cannot be assumed, especially in this case with Christian and Boy—their age difference and both being male.

Unsure of what would happen, excited but apprehensive, we drove innocent Christian up to George's camp. He followed us into the first compound, and in the other one we saw Katania and Boy. Katania was tiny and cute, but our attention was riveted by Boy. He was enormous, impressive, and stood motionless with his eyes on Christian, who was instantly aware of his presence but, understandably confused and frightened, unwilling to even look at him. We walked toward Bill and George, who were standing a few yards from the dividing wire fence. Christian was reluctant to follow, but slowly picked his way toward us, his eyes averted from Boy. Bewildered, he crouched behind us, pressed against our legs. Katania sensed the impending events and wisely kept well away. Suddenly, with a deafening roar, Boy ferociously charged at

Christian. Under his weight the wire gave slightly, and we all scattered. Poor Christian remained where he was, but cringed and snarled. Momentarily satisfied, Boy walked away. Christian was badly shaken and needed consoling. He leaned on our legs and sat on our feet, insistent we did not leave him. It was obviously a shock for him to discover that he was not the only lion in the world, and worse, that the first one he met was at least twice his size. We waited a few yards from the wire for about half an hour. Boy kept a nonchalant eye on Christian, who either sat on us or hid behind our legs pretending to be asleep. Several more times Boy charged at Christian, who again cowered and snarled.

We moved away from the wire, the initial introduction over. Boy had behaved predictably, for as an adult lion he demanded submission from Christian, but George noted that Christian, too, had behaved predictably and correctly, cowering and deferring to an older male. Christian was very nervous all day, and although his eyes were constantly on Boy, he stayed close to us, well away from the wire. That night we put a bed for him between our beds, but our sleep was broken by Boy's powerful, haunting roars, which frightened Christian and us equally.

Christian spent most of the next day on George's bed, although he was free to leave the compound if he wished. We were rather worried about him as he seemed too at home on the bed and appeared to take no interest in Boy or Katania. He occasionally gave them a cool glance in the next compound. But late in the afternoon he walked to within a few yards of the dividing fence. Katania came over and flirted with him. Christian was definitely interested but did not move any closer. Boy charged toward him, and again Christian cowered. He then casually retreated and came back to us, and we felt that he had made a positive step.

The following morning George constructed a small hatch between the two compounds so that Katania could be with either Boy or Christian. The crucial introduction would be between Boy and

Christian, but Katania could be a helpful link. She tentatively came through the hatch twice, but Christian was of course asleep on a bed and did not see her. Again we were concerned about Christian's lack of interest in communicating with them. He pretended they did not exist, but we sensed he knew exactly what their movements were.

Later we took him for a walk, and he seemed relieved to be away from Boy and Katania. The countryside stretched endlessly, broken only occasionally by outcrops of rock. George had chosen the campsite for a variety of reasons, but Kora Rock, the large rock outcrop overlooking the camp, was ideal for the lions to use for observation. It was unattractive here in comparison with the Tana River, but still rather beautiful—various shades of gray and brown, and splashes of green around dried-up water holes. Barren, and mainly covered by low, thick thornbushes, it was a harsh area for the lions to live in. Christian had come to what could be described as another "World's End."

Back in the camp he teased the Africans constructing the huts; he bit a few bottoms and knee-caps, and jumped on whatever they happened to be carrying. These Africans adjusted to Christian but were always wary of him, as lions are their traditional enemies. George was interested to see that Christian, unlike most other lions, showed no color prejudice. Boy, who would accept Europeans, growled fiercely each time an African came too close to his compound, but Christian did not share this dislike and amused us all for the afternoon. He seemed a travesty of a lion.

In high spirits, Christian now became rather provocative with Boy. He focused his attention almost entirely on him, and a little later he strode boldly up to the dividing wire and lay down. Boy charged and Christian turned and fled. But he came back a few minutes later and appeared to be teasing Boy, who was outraged by this impudence and again charged angrily. Christian even poked his head through Katania's hatch, but hastily withdrew it when Boy spotted him. Perhaps he had tired of having no contact with them, yet strangely it still seemed more natural for Christian to be with humans rather than lions. We certainly appeared to appreciate him more.

The next day George decided that it was time for Christian to meet Katania, who had been unwilling to leave Boy and come through the hatch to Christian. It was unusual for a fully grown lion and a four-month-old lioness to have such a strong, affectionate relationship because in a natural pride the adult lion has little contact with the cubs. But since they had been living together at Naivasha, Boy, probably to his embarrassment, had been cast in the role of mother-substitute.

George led Boy out of his compound, and Christian, safely on the other side of the wire, stalked him as he walked past. Boy rushed at the fence, but his charges now seemed less convincing, and we suspected that he was rapidly becoming bored with this necessary display of authority. Interestingly, when he charged this time, Christian snarled as usual, but for the first time rolled over on his back, the gesture of submission from the younger lion that Boy demanded.

With Boy outside we could then take Christian through a gate into the other compound. He walked up to the other end, where Katania was pacing, distressed by her separation from Boy. Christian approached her confidently, and they exchanged a beautiful greeting, their heads gently touching. He was intrigued and continually licked and smelled her. Boy jealously watched all this from outside, but after an initial charge at the fence to demonstrate his disapproval, he appeared resigned.

Christian and Katania played together, and although he was much bigger he was very gentle, and she squealed on the few occasions he was too rough with her. He followed her, tapping her back legs and tripping her. This was a game that he and Unity had devised at Leith Hill. Christian was delighted to have a lion to play with, and afterward we thought that he was rather smug and offhand with us!

Boy was led back into our compound, and Katania ran through the hatch to greet him. After smelling her he grimaced, baring his teeth to show his displeasure at Christian's scent, but another step had been taken. We were very uneasy about Boy spending the night in our compound with us, as we had not been introduced to him either. To our horror he chose to sleep in our tent, and we did not dare argue. This really unnerved us. We did not know him and he did not know us. We were associated with Christian, who as a young male must have appeared as a threat to him. On several occasions he gently raised our arms up in his huge jaws and teeth and it was hard not to panic. Unexpected quick movements can alarm and frighten lions, with dangerous consequences, and we tried to appear relaxed and not radiate any fear. He urinated where he liked, staking out his territory, and we just tiptoed around him. We found Boy quite unknowable and privately felt he had had too many injuries, operations, and anesthetics.

On the following day George thought that enough

time had elapsed for Christian to be safely introduced to Boy outside the compound. It was a meeting we had all waited for anxiously, but aware that if
there was a fight between them, Christian had no
chance. The decision was George's, and we relied
on his experience and judgement. We led Christian
up onto Kora Rock behind the camp where he
wanted them to meet. Then George led Boy and
Katania up from a different direction. Boy and Katania lay down about fifteen yards from Christian,
who was watching intently. For twenty minutes we
stood nervously and watched and waited. Although
impatient to make contact with Boy, Christian
correctly sensed that it was not for him to make the
first move.

Katania finally became bored with the tense situation and wandered toward Christian, and they
greeted one another. Boy immediately stood up and
charged at him. It was a very frightening moment,
intensified by their roars and snarls. Christian
rolled over on his back submissively, and, satisfied,

Boy lay down a few yards from him. Although they appeared to be fighting savagely, with paws and legs flailing, very little physical contact had been made, and Christian seemed to be unhurt.

After an interval of about ten minutes, Katania, who had wisely run off during the encounter, again came over to Christian and triggered off another frightening performance. This time Boy walked away, leaving Christian badly shaken and looking miserable. He then came over to us and, comforting him, we walked back to camp, noting a few scratches and a slight limp.

Although it was an orchestrated situation, we had witnessed a natural introduction between an adult lion and a younger lion. If Christian had been any older, Boy would probably have killed him as a potential threat to his position. Despite our feelings for Christian, we felt we were intruders in animal society and their protocol. Christian had instinctively known what his role was, and he had followed the conventions of the lion world by his submission. George commented that Christian had shown considerable courage by his determination to face Boy and not flee from him. Christian was obviously growing fond of Katania, but it was Boy's acceptance he was so anxious to win. To gain this, he had to endure some ongoing unpleasant but necessary formalities.

We could now all live in the same compound. Over the next few days, Christian stayed as close to Boy as he would permit. If Christian was too daring, Boy would charge, but the charges had lost their intensity. Christian concentrated adoringly on Boy and even imitated his movements; he followed him around, sat down when he sat down, and lay in the same position. We often saw him lying just around a corner from Boy, a clever trick to get closer to him than would normally be allowed. He sometimes played with Katania, but she was a poor second to Boy. Christian was still affectionate toward us, but he was definitely a lion's lion.

Each morning we went walking with George and

the lions until they chose some shade in which to spend the hottest hours of the day. Christian followed behind Boy and Katania, but sat down and looked in another direction whenever Boy noticed him. In the afternoons we would find the three lions together, but Christian was always a few yards away, not yet an accepted member of the pride.

We had an extraordinary human-animal coexistence living with the lions at Kora. It was a potentially very dangerous environment, totally reliant on George's experience and knowledge of lion behavior. George's confidence in both lions and humans was sometimes questioned over the years by his detractors, but overall, his faith had been justified. We spent ridiculous nights with the three lions often in our tent. While Katania bit our toes or stole our blankets, Christian hid under a bed, and Boy roared thunderously, followed by any number of defiant grunts.

After a few days Boy greeted us in the same way he greeted George, and his huge head would rub up against us. He had a seemingly placid nature, but a total assumption of superiority. Like all cats, everything had to be his idea, and he did only what he wanted to do. Filming had continued at Kora, and we often had to wait hours until Boy was suitably positioned. In contrast we just carried Christian into the correct position, or simply rolled him over to face the cameras. We found ourselves describing Boy as a "marvelous" lion, and physically he was, but compared with Christian's youthful exuberance, he seemed to have less personality. Our praise of Boy was really just relief that he had eaten neither us nor Christian.

Christian had now been in Africa for several weeks. He was tougher and his pads had hardened and he was growing into a very handsome lion. Bill described him as the "Jean-Paul Belmondo of the lion world," referring to a French film star of the time. Christian had always been healthy, but one day he was suddenly listless. We thought he might be depressed by Boy's reluctance to fully accept him, but because of the whiteness of his gums and his hot nose, George took his temperature and diagnosed tick fever. Christian had no immunity against this disease, and George, fortunately anticipating it, was able to inject him with the appropriate vaccine. He believed that Elsa had died from tick fever, and that if he had had this vaccine then, he might have saved her. Christian was very sick for two days but quickly recovered.

Now that Christian had been introduced to Boy, Bill and the film crew returned to England to edit the film. George suggested that we should also leave Kora for a short time so that Christian could get used to life without us. We decided to visit other parts of Kenya and Tanzania before returning to say good-bye.

11

Onward Christian

In Kenya we visited the Maasai Mara, and in Tanzania the Serengeti, Lake Manyara, and Ngorongoro Crater. We saw a variety of animals such as wildebeest, zebra, antelope, herds of elephant, cheetah, leopard, and huge flocks of birds like flamingos, often in spectacular surroundings. We were most impressed by the dramatically beautiful Ngorongoro Crater, and for the first time met some of the elegant Maasai people, who have staunchly defended their right to a traditional lifestyle with their cattle, even more threatened today by the competition for land and resources. It was there that we saw our first lions in the wild: three cubs and two lionesses. While tourism is an important industry and gives employment to many Africans, there was something disturbing about "wild" lions that appeared unconcerned by the Land Rovers that totally encircled them, and the tourists leaning out of the windows taking photographs. One woman in a game reserve who had been driven by a guide to see the unusual sight of a lion guarding his freshly killed buffalo from vultures said, "I've come to see kills, not carcasses. Drive on."

Conditions in the lodges where we stayed varied from nights under canvas to the luxurious. All the lodges were expensive and full of enthusiastic middle-aged tourists, who seemed to feel that the cost of their African holiday was justified if they saw one lion. While these tourists were obviously loving their African experience and expanding their awareness of animals in the wild, we were less easily satisfied, having flown with our own lion to Africa. We had been spoiled by our weeks at Kora, living with several lions, and at a pace at which it was possible to absorb a deep feeling for Africa. Rather than have many animals paraded before us, we preferred to see a few of them unexpectedly, or to sit quietly by the Tana River for hours watching the shy waterbucks, baboons, oryx, and elephants come warily for their evening drink.

We decided to visit Joy Adamson at Elsamere, her house on the shores of Lake Naivasha, a drive of one and a half hours from Nairobi. Prior to relocating to Kora, George had been staying there monitoring Boy's recovery from his injuries and operations.

Joy Adamson was born in Austria and first went to Africa in 1936, where she met her second husband, Peter Bally, a botanist. Joy was a very talented woman with great enthusiasms, often allied to her partners' occupations. She was a very fine botanical artist, and also painted many animals, birds, and a definitive series on the tribes of Kenya, which are in the Nairobi Museum. Joy and George first met in 1942 and had a volatile marriage and relationship up until her death.

After Elsa the lion cub was raised and rehabilitated by them, their lives were devoted to the conservation of animals and returning different species to the wild. Joy wrote *Born Free* from George's diaries, which was published in 1960 and followed by a film version in 1966. Both were huge worldwide hits.

Joy had set up The Elsa Wild Animal Appeal in 1961, which is now called The Elsa Conservation Trust. The documentary about Christian's rehabilitation and the allotment of Kora for this purpose gave George financial independence from Joy for the first time and a place to live with his lions. Joy resented this, so it was with some trepidation that we drove up to Elsamere, where to our surprise the sofas were upholstered in lion skins. When we dared ask her about them, she brushed our concerns aside with, "There are good lions and bad lions."

Despite her reputation for being difficult and

Left: George, Ace, Christian, and John rest in the shade at George's camp.

Bottom: Christian's first night in the African bush, and a reassuring paw on John's face.

Top: A terrifying moment as Boy charges the wire, establishing his dominance over Christian.

Above: The dramatic first meeting of Boy and Christian outside the compound.

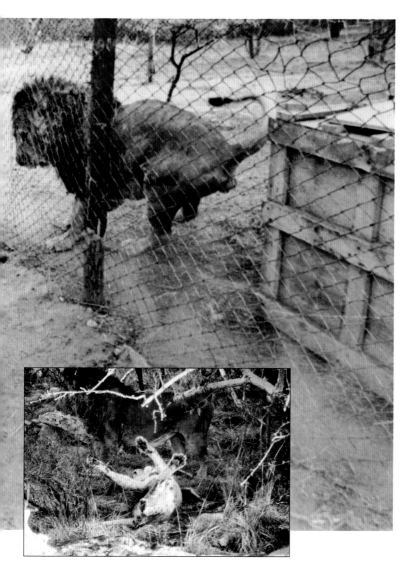

Fortunately, Christian reacted correctly and submissively and suffered only a few scratches.

THE REUNION IN 1971

Above: Christian running toward Ace and John when he recognizes them.

Top left: Jumping up to greet Ace and John.

Far right: Christian had doubled in size in the year since Ace and John had seen him.

In 1972, Ace and John returned to see Christian. He had again doubled in size but still remembered them and greeted them with the same affection.

John and Ace with Christian on the rock overlooking George's camp.

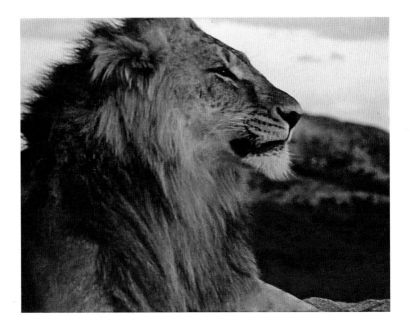

frequently falling out with people, she was reasonably friendly with us, intelligent, and interesting, and curious about Christian's background. She was relieved to hear that Boy was recovering from his injuries, although he was still limping. She was skeptical about Christian's chances of surviving in the wild. "Your stupid fat English lion will be killed, and so will George," she said. Joy was very keen to visit Kora but was annoyed at being excluded from the work there. Despite the huge earnings from *Born Free*, she never financially supported George's work. When she did visit Kora she was very anxious to be photographed with Christian, but subsequently declared, "It is time for humans to leave the lions alone." This was the conundrum of their lives: the success of their work and the independence and self-sufficiency of the animals made them redundant.

Like some people who love animals, she did not see the irony in her often disastrous human relationships or her reputation for harshness with her African staff. She was murdered by one of them in 1980 after a dispute about pay.

On our way through Nairobi, we took a sample of Christian's blood to the vets, Tony and Sue Harthoorn. George had correctly diagnosed tick fever, and the vets told us that there was a slight chance that it would recur, but George had the correct vaccine to combat it. Boy and Katania were also susceptible to this disease just by moving from one part of Kenya to another.

On the long drive back we lost our way in the darkness and were alarmed when our Land Rover was flagged down by what looked like almost-naked, spear-holding warriors. We thought we should stop, but quickly wound up the windows. We were embarrassed to see they were friendly young African children with sticks, merely wanting cigarettes. In English, they directed us to Kora and "Kampi ya Simba, where the white man keeps lions!"

We arrived at George's camp late that night. He was concerned about Christian, who for the first time had not returned with Boy and Katania in the evening. George had looked for him and called him, but he had not appeared.

Within several minutes of our arrival, however, Christian came running toward the camp. We had been away for a fortnight and, wildly excited, he leapt all over us. George believed he must have had a premonition that we were returning. He thinks lions have a sixth sense that humans have either lost or never had. On visits to his other lions after their release in the wild, he has often arrived in a deserted camp only to be mysteriously joined by them a few minutes later.

Christian had obviously missed us and made continuous happy grunts while leaping on us and licking our faces. When we sat down, he would clamber onto one of our laps, then stretch to have at least part of his body, his front paws, on the other lap. He excitedly jumped on the table, creating chaos and making eating impossible, and we were not allowed to sleep.

We were delighted to see he looked so well and that George was growing fond of him and found him as amusing as we did. One night George had unwisely made Christian a snack of powdered milk, a great favorite from his English days. And now, every night, Christian followed him around, tapping his ankles and butting him with his head, until he relented and gave him his powdered milk.

Disappointingly, Boy had still not totally accepted Christian, although there had been an improvement. George thought Christian sometimes seemed depressed by his unrequited adoration of Boy. He and Katania were now very friendly, and George thought that now it might be Boy's jealousy that was prolonging the ongoing tension.

He told us of an incident that had happened the day we left Kora. He had followed the lions on their morning walk, and he had seen an enormous rhinoceros quite close to the camp. Boy and Katania tactfully moved well away from it. But to George's alarm, Christian began to walk toward the rhinoceros. He stalked it perfectly and came to within a few yards, when the rhinoceros suddenly turned and saw him, and snorting with rage at Christian's impudence, charged. Christian sprang eight feet in the air, over a bush, and fled. George was very amused, but hoped Christian had learned his lesson.

Already Boy had spent several nights away in an attempt to establish a territory. He chose the opposite direction from a wild lion heard roaring on several occasions. However, it was impossible for a single fully grown lion to establish a territory alone, and George told us he planned to bring two other lions up to the camp. He had been offered two lionesses of about Christian's age, which had been captured after they had frequently attacked domestic cattle, and without George's intervention, they would have been killed.

This time we spent only a few days with George and Christian. Each morning we walked with the lions until they chose a tree or bush in order to shelter from the sun. Christian always accompanied Boy and Katania, but Boy suffered his presence rather than encouraged it. In the afternoons we walked with George to find them, fascinated by the way he could identify and follow their spoor (paw marks), and by his deep knowledge of wildlife and bushcraft. The lions returned in the evenings to be fed, and George sometimes had to drive many miles to a hunting block to shoot waterbuck or other game for them to eat. He hoped they would soon be self-sufficient.

We loved talking to George and had long conversations with him, not only about lions but also about Australia and our lives in London, and his life. George had been born in 1906 in India, where his father was in the British Army, and he was educated in England. He had spent most of his life as a game warden with the Department of Wildlife in Kenya. Although he led an isolated life, George kept in touch with events in the outside world. He had returned to England only once since leaving school, and he was interested to hear how London had changed now so many years later. He was kept informed by visitors, friends, and admirers around the world, as well as by *Playboy* magazine, which he read "for the interviews."

He talked of his early days as a hunter and when he first realized the threat of extinction that faced so many animals, he had become increasingly concerned for their conservation. Since Elsa's death he had devoted his life to rehabilitating lions.

George loved lions passionately, and believed it was possible to attain an understanding and communication with them that was less likely, if not impossible, with other animals. He admired their dignity and immense capacity for love and trust, and he wanted to continue living at Kampa ya Simba until the lions were no longer dependent on him.

He felt Boy was about to grant Christian the acceptance he longed for, and that the other lions, in addition to easing the situation, would complete the nucleus of a pride that would include Christian. He was confident that all the lions would be successfully rehabilitated.

Through a series of extraordinary coincidences we had returned Christian to Africa and to the world's most knowledgeable and sympathetic lion expert. Christian now had the freedom to take his chance in the wild, and we could not have imagined or dreamed of a better outcome and this tempered our sadness at leaving him. Life would initially be very empty without him, and tears were shed. We wondered if we would ever see him again, but Christian, after a journey of several generations and thousands of miles, had returned to where he belonged.

12

Christian's Progress

Several months after we left Kora and returned to London, we had news of Christian, Boy, and Katania in a letter from George, part of which follows:

I expect you have heard about the tragedy of poor little Katania. One evening last month the three lions pushed off towards the river after having a good feed of meat. They did not return the following morning, which was nothing unusual, as on several occasions they had been absent for two or three days, once even for five days. I went searching for them two days later but without success. In the early hours of the next day Christian appeared alone. This was a little worrying as usually he and Katania kept together, while Boy went off looking for girls. However, I thought Katania must surely be with Boy. Early next morning Boy arrived, alone.

Now there was real cause for alarm, and Christian seemed just as worried as I was. I started an intensive search on foot and by Land Rover. I took Christian walking with me, relying on his powers of scent for help. It was not until four days later that I found the spoor of the three lions on the bank of the river, about three miles below where you stayed by the Tana before moving up to my camp. It was plain to see that Christian and Katania had been playing, racing up and down along the bank. I crossed to the far bank but found Boy's tracks only. On the near side, there were only the tracks of Christian leaving the river. I think Katania must have tried to follow Boy into the water, but being so much lighter and smaller, was carried down by the current, and before she could make the bank, she was taken by a crocodile. Even at her age lions are very good swimmers and it is unlikely that she would have drowned. It is a sad loss which I feel keenly, as do Boy and Christian. The joy has gone out of them.

About a fortnight ago, Boy went off on another foray across the river and returned with a girl-friend. I could hear them around the camp for three days and nights. One night while Boy was busy with his lioness, I heard Christian growling near the edge of the bush in front of the camp. By the light of a torch, I saw him facing another wild lioness of about his own age.

Boy and Christian are now good friends. In fact, Boy often takes the initiative in the greeting ritual of mutual head rubbing. Christian has started to accompany Boy in his roaring! A trifle immature, but a darned good effort. His voice promises to be even deeper than Boy's. A few days ago, there is reason to think that the two met up with the lionesses again, who may have made a kill, as both returned looking well fed and not in the least hungry after three days.

I soon hope to collect the lionesses that you know about. From the description given to me, I would say they are about fourteen months old, which means that they should have already had experience of hunting with their mother. They should be a big asset, provided I can gain their trust and friendship.

George Adamson
January 12, 1971
Kampi ya Simba, Kora

Bill Travers flew out to Kenya shortly after we received this news from George and wrote to us on his return to England:

Dear John and Ace,
I arrived back from Africa at the week-end. I can imagine your concern over the past weeks and thirst for news of Christian, so before I go into details of how he is making out, let me tell you first

of all that he is both alive and well. He does not seem to have had a day's sickness since the tick fever he had when you were both out there. And he is very much alive I can assure you—my paw-marked khaki trousers will bear witness to that. He is a good deal heavier too, well over 200 lbs I would say at a guess, though sometimes when he greeted me fondly it felt considerably more. I am quite sure we could never now lift and suspend him from the local butcher's scales as we once did in England to find out his exact weight for the flight to Kenya, even if he would still allow it. He is as high at the shoulder as any fully grown lion, even as tall as Boy who, as you know, is a big lion. But in spite of his size he is as affectionate as ever. He gives George long ceremonial greetings with his head, licks him with his sandpaper tongue the moment George puts a foot outside the wire fencing that runs round the camp, inside which Christian is now no longer allowed.

However, this affection does not seem to be hampering the progress of rehabilitation, but in a strange way gives George the control that he will continue to need during the months that it takes to establish the lions first as a family and then as guardians of their territory.

By the way, I noticed that his coat seems to have adjusted to the hotter climate and is thinner, much finer and smoother, which makes him look more streamlined, more mature and certainly emphasises his now fine athletic figure. He is really quite a magnificent lion, and it would be hard to find anything to criticise in his appearance, except perhaps his feet. They are still enormous. I can only think if he grows big enough to make them look normal he will be, without doubt, the biggest lion in Africa.

After you left Boy and Christian became the greatest of friends—in fact quite inseparable, and the little cub Katania, who as you saw adored them both, found herself as they flopped over each other, the protesting centre of a sandwich.

Unfortunately, this friendship, as you have already been told, was short-lived. I won't therefore dwell on the circumstances which led us to assume the death of Katania, except to say it was doubly tragic. Not only had Boy and Christian lost their little friend, we'd also lost the only female in George's pride.

However, there is good news too, to compensate. The two lionesses George has collected are about the right age for Christian—a few months younger than he is. Unlike Christian they are already quite wild, and though too young to kill must have learned from their parents how to hunt. They must also have some knowledge of the strict rules of lion society. I think Christian will benefit greatly from his association with them as the pavements of Chelsea and the soft country life at our home were hardly the best schooling for the life he is now starting to lead. The other good part of this news is that they are female. George, of course, is delighted as it is essential to have at least one female in the family or pride which we hope eventually will be able, with George's help, to establish itself in the Tana River area and enjoy freedom and a natural expression of life.

Well, I am sure there can hardly be a day that you do not talk or at least think about Christian,

George and Boy. I can only tell you that the last picture I took with me, as I drove away from George's camp, was one of the three friends standing happily together for a final word outside the gate of their "home." A pat, a handshake, and they remained watching my Land Rover as it started bumping down the long trail back to Nairobi and civilisation. I looked back as often as I dared take my eyes off the road and saw Christian rub against George, who fondled his slight mane, then wander off to Boy, to greet, nudge and no doubt provoke him into starting some wonderful sprawling lion game.

I felt strangely happy. I think if it were not for George Adamson and for people such as yourselves, Christian would have ended up in very different circumstances. . . .

All the best,

Yours,

Bill

13

❋

The YouTube Reunion,
1971

After Boy and Christian's first dramatic encounters and prolonged standoff, they finally became inseparable, particularly after the death of Katania.

In his 1985 autobiography *My Pride and Joy,* George described the early days at Kora with Boy and Christian as "some of the most enjoyable of my life." The wild lions, however, resented the intrusion into their territory by Boy, Christian, and the two lionesses, Monalisa and Juma, that had arrived from Maralal in northeastern Kenya. As the only mature lion and head of the pride, Boy had frequent confrontations with these wild lions. One day Boy returned to camp with deep wounds on his back, and George treated them in the safety of the compound. The wild lions waited expectantly outside, and unable to get at Boy, they attacked and killed Monalisa.

Boy seemed to be in great pain from this latest injury and now wandered off more frequently on his own, leaving Juma and Christian, who had become good friends, unprotected. George was becoming increasingly concerned about Boy's well-being.

George was then given two eighteen-month-old lionesses from the Nairobi Park Orphanage, which he named Mona and Lisa (in memory of Monalisa), and a boisterous young male called Supercub. George's plans to create a self-sufficient pride were progressing, with Christian an integral part of the pride.

But George's plans and Christian's rehabilitation suffered a tragic setback. On June 6, 1971, Boy had been away for a few days, and the other lions were on Kora Rock behind the camp. George realized Boy had returned when he heard him drinking from the water trough outside the camp compound. Suddenly George heard cries from the same direction, and, grabbing his gun, ran out to see Boy with his assistant, Stanley, in his jaws. George shouted at Boy, who dropped Stanley. George shot Boy dead. He then rushed to Stanley's assistance, but he died almost immediately.

George was devastated. Stanley had been instructed not to go outside the compound, but he had ignored this advice and now he had lost his life. George also mourned one of his favorite lions, whose life had been intertwined with his own since Boy was a cub. The "accident," as it came to be called, made international news and was fully investigated by the local police and the Game Department. George's work was criticized for endangering lives, and the whole project was temporarily at risk. However, George had many supporters, including government ministers who appreciated the value of the Adamson name to Kenyan tourism, and he was allowed to remain at Kora.

We had been living in London writing *A Lion Called Christian,* which was due for publication in November 1971. We had intended to fly to Kenya and visit Christian with a film crew, as they had nearly completed the second documentary, *Christian the Lion,* and wanted to include Christian's reunion with us nearly one year later. With George's shocking news, we delayed the visit a few weeks.

When we arrived in Nairobi, we were told by various people that there were rumors that Boy had always been the least predictable of the Adamson lions, and that Stanley had been disrespectful and careless around Boy on several occasions.

We flew from Wilson Airport in Nairobi, and when we landed on the earth strip Terence Adamson had cleared a few miles from the camp at Kora,

George was waiting to meet us. He was looking well, considering the tragedy, and we hoped our visit was to be a diversion for him. We tried not to bombard him with questions about Christian as we drove back to Kampi ya Simba. Although George had not seen the lions for a while, they had just appeared that morning and were now resting from the heat in the shade. We anxiously waited in the now much more comfortable and permanent camp. We could only guess at the reception we would get from Christian, but we felt deep inside that it could only be a loving one, and that he could not have forgotten us. Could a year apart have changed our relationship?

Ace described the reunion in a letter written to his parents at the time:

The lions were "lying up" about half a mile away, and we had to impatiently wait several hours until it was less hot and the lions would be likely to move. Finally, with the film crew, we walked in the direction of the lions, and waited at the base of Kora

Rock while George went over the top to call Christian. Shortly afterwards Christian appeared at the
top—about 75 yards away from us. He stared hard
at us for a few seconds, and then slowly moved
closer for a good look. He stared intently. He
looked marvellous, and up on the rocks, he didn't
appear much bigger. We couldn't wait any longer
and called him. He immediately started to run
down towards us. Grunting with excitement, this
ENORMOUS lion jumped all over us, but he was
very gentle. Soon we had 3 lionesses milling around
us—about Christian's age but not nearly as big.
And Supercub, a delightful 5 month old male.
Quite unforgettable of course. Christian showed
his affection in exactly the same way, had all his old
tricks & some new ones. George is just captivated
by him—as everyone is. He is the best natured lion
George has seen—with humans and lions. He is in
superb condition—much sleeker, and because of
the heat his mane hasn't grown much. His spots
have finally faded more. His front teeth are a
frightening 1 1/2 inches of white ivory! It was dif-

ficult to adjust to his size—he was about 160 lbs 10 months ago, now George thinks he is about 300 lbs. We gave him enormous respect, and were a little less frivolous with him—a much more mature lion, but still most entertaining. Undoubtedly head of the pride—he rather enjoyed playing out the role for us. George is delighted with their progress—they have become a "tight unit," and apparently they could begin to kill quite soon, which sounds bloody, but will be essential for their survival.

Nairobi 20/7/71

Reading these words again so many years later, like looking at the reunion footage, brings back so many memories of what was undoubtedly one of the most extraordinary days of our lives. Although it was nearly a year later, George had had complete confidence Christian would remember us, and that we would be safe. We instinctively felt this too. We know people expect us to have been frightened, but we had no fear of him. We knew Christian so well and could read his behavior, and had built up such trust with him. But could this have changed? We were so excited at the thought of seeing him, but there was also some anxiety, as no one could really predict what would actually happen. Any doubts dissolved as Christian, once he had ascertained it was us and we called his name, ran toward us with such enthusiasm and affection, making his excited little grunts with a loving expression we recognized. As this now much bigger and even more handsome lion ran toward us, our only concern was could we physically handle the joyous leaping upon us and hugs we now knew were inevitable. He was surprisingly gentle with us under the circumstances, and we were all surprised at just how exuberant this welcome was, and we were just ecstatic. We weren't even frightened of the other lions who had materialized and were now milling around our legs, and although Mona, Lisa, Juma, and Supercub had had very little human contact, the atmosphere was so infectious that they too were just as caught up in it.

We were woken by Christian's roars each morning, and they were impressive for a three-year-old. We spent the next few days enjoying George's normal camp routine, walking with the lions in the morning, sometimes sitting with Christian in the shade while they dozed, or setting out with George in the late afternoon to find them. Now, a few weeks after the death of Boy, Christian was relishing his position as head of the pride. We let Christian totally dictate our relationship with him. If he wanted to play we played, and if he wanted to be affectionate we reciprocated. At other times we were superfluous to his life or a distraction and we just left him alone.

It was fun and challenging getting to know the other lions, who were virtually wild and had all arrived at Kora very wary of humans. Looking back now at this lion-human interaction, we wonder if George possibly had too much confidence in all of us. One day Christian was leading us on a walk when he suddenly charged off into the bush with a huge growl, chasing after Mona and Lisa. They had been crouched waiting in ambush for us, probably for fun, but this could have been a very dangerous encounter if we had reacted with fear or been knocked over. We were very touched by Christian's protective attitude. Lisa was a very playful lioness, Supercub had a very extroverted personality, but Juma and Mona were both very shy. In a letter to Sir William Collins, George wrote that, ironically, Christian, the lion from London that had the most contact with humans, was the easiest lion to rehabilitate at Kora so far.

Kampi ya Simba had much improved in the last year. George's brother Terence had built a number of permanent huts with palm-leaf roofs and walls, ingeniously made from chicken wire covered with burlap and then painted with numerous coats of cement. The largest of these simple but effective buildings was the mess hut, which was the hub of the camp and where George kept the radio telephone, his only link with the outside world. He also had an ancient typewriter and a jumble of books, letters, diaries, and photographs. There was now a generator to power the deep freezers, which were mostly stacked with camel meat for the lions, purchased from the nearest village, Asako, forty miles away. George's cook, Hamisi, cooked for us on an open fire in his own lion-proof compound.

There was now a menagerie surrounding the camp, including noisy guinea fowl, ravens, friendly hornbills, monitor lizards, the occasional unwelcome snakes and scorpions, and the ever-waiting vultures that Christian was always chasing away from his old bones.

While it was a unique experience to visit Kampi ya Simba, we only planned to stay a few days because the less contact the lions had with humans the better. Visitors to the camp were often disappointed when George would not allow them to approach his lions, so we were very privileged. The lions had to be self-sufficient and were encouraged to be wary of humans.

We had been welcomed by Christian in the most wonderful, loving, unforgettable way. That day was a euphoric experience for all of us, lions and people. Now, via YouTube nearly forty years later, that experience has been shared by millions of people all over the world.

We were obviously sad to leave Christian, but he seemed so contented and everything was going well at the moment. The wild lions had been quiet for a while, and there was a calmness at Kora. When we left and our small plane circled the camp, Christian and the other lions looked up from Kora Rock, and as one of us waved back to George in the compound, the other shed a few quiet tears. In this unpredictable and often hostile environment, would Christian's good fortune continue?

14

The Final Farewell,

1972

In London we were kept informed of any news, and in January 1972 we received two letters from Kora. George wrote:

I have been very lucky in finding a young man to help me. Tony Fitzjohn, aged about 27. A bit of a wanderer who has tried his hand at many occupations. Very fit and capable.

A letter also came to us from Tony, who had originally written to Joy Adamson asking for a job, but she had suggested he work for George. She felt he needed an enthusiastic and multiskilled young helper.

Dear Ace and John,
Although we've never met I thought I'd put a few lines down.
    I've been helping George for some time and have become as fond of Christian as you must have been. It is amazing to see how he's adapted himself to the wild here yet remains as completely attached to George as ever.

It was excellent news that George had more support, and we planned to visit again later in the year.

But further letters informed us that life was quite difficult for Christian and the other lions. Without Boy, Christian on his own had not been able to defend the territory around the camp, and a wild lion known as "The Killer" had killed the engaging Supercub.

Christian had survived his fights with wild lions so far, and George noted that his wounds were always on his forelegs and shoulders which demonstrated that he had been fighting courageously.

In another letter George wrote:

> Christian had had a fight with a wild lion and had two nasty gashes in his right foreleg. But he did not seem the least perturbed about his encounter and it was with much difficulty that I persuaded him to follow me back to camp, where I could attend to his injuries.

Christian was proving to be an exceptionally well adapted and brave young lion in this hostile environment, but growing frustrations became evident that could have had catastrophic consequences. One day he ambushed and knocked George over, held him with his paws, and had his head in his jaws. Christian released him quickly and George chased after him with a stick. Luckily, George was not badly hurt, although a claw had punctured his arm. Christian knew he had "broken the rules," but soon after he also knocked Tony down several times, cuffed him with his paws, and with his head in his jaws dragged him by the head. Tony punched Christian hard on the nose, and was immediately released, and amazingly was not badly injured either.

We were shocked when we heard about these incidents. Christian could have killed them if he wanted to, or killed them accidentally by seemingly minor wounds. George and Tony felt that Christian was frustrated, adolescent, and lonely, and in a territory where he may never be able to live or establish a pride. The lionesses had mated with the wild lions, and while this was ideal for their rehabilitation, it left Christian on his own. While we sympathized with Christian's situation, we thought George and Tony's attitude was magnanimous. We appreciated how unique and fortunate our relationship had been with Christian, who in very unnatural circumstances in England had never attacked anyone.

Now that he was adolescent and stronger, would our relationship with him change? How would he now react with other visitors to Kora?

In August 1972, over a year since our reunion, we asked George if we could visit him and Christian and meet Tony Fitzjohn. He responded enthusiastically but warned that he could not guarantee Christian would be around camp because the wild lions had driven him farther up the Tana River, and he often spent weeks away. Nevertheless, we decided to go, as there was never any certainty that George could remain at Kora, and there might not be another opportunity.

Tony met us in Nairobi, and we immediately saw what an asset he must have been at Kampi ya Simba and why George liked him so much. It is remarkable to think that today, so many years later, he is continuing George's conservation work at Mkomazi

National Park in Tanzania and is the Field Director of the George Adamson Wildlife Preservation
Trust.

We arrived at the camp to find George with flu
but happy to see us, especially as we came with whis-
key and gin. He had been hearing Christian mating
with a wild lioness, and it was not until the third
night that to our great relief he appeared. Although
he did not jump up on us like before, his greeting
was as exuberant and as physical. He was just as
vocal, although his excited grunts were now much
deeper. But he was enormous, and milling between
us he knocked over George, who was not amused.

George believed that Christian was possibly the
largest lion in Kenya, and certainly the largest lion
in the immediate Tana area. He estimated his weight
as close to five hundred pounds, though he was still
only three years old and would continue to grow.

Over dinner we listened to George and Tony's
accounts of Christian's adventures, his fights with
the wild lions, his frustrations and assertiveness,
and their accounts and interpretation of Christian's

attack on them both. They both loved him and did not bear any resentment over what they described as his adolescent frustration. We sat up talking all night with Christian interrupting us, entertaining us, and trying to push us off our chairs.

Ace also wrote to his parents about this visit to Christian.

> We saw Christian every morning & evening for a walk and a chat. He is much calmer & much more self assured than last year, and stunning to be with. Just as silly. Huge. Jumped up on me only once as before on his hind legs and he did it extremely gently. He licked my face as he towered over me. He nearly crushed John by trying to sit on his lap!

Over the next few days we observed how much he had matured. While happy to greet us, he was even more independent than he was the last year. He dictated when he wanted to be with us and for how long, and he spent a lot of time outside the compound. Again we had absolutely no fear of him, and looking back at the footage of the time, we seem to be constantly patting and talking to him, which he handled very patiently.

George was delighted by Christian's progress and he was obviously a favorite. Christian had now fully accepted Tony, who had never worked with lions before. Tony was to become an expert in bushcraft, and his diverse technical and mechanical skills were invaluable at Kampi ya Simba and greatly improved their communication with the world.

This time we stayed nine days and saw more of the surrounding countryside. We went fishing with Terence, who often provided a welcome addition of fresh fish for the camp. He was an expert on plant life, and he pointed out among the thornbushes and acacias the more exotic myrrh and frankincense shrubs. To us, the shapes of many of the plants and the washed-out colors looked different from the equivalent semi-arid bush areas in Australia, but both continents have a lot in common: a wide variety of climates and vegetations, open spaces, a far horizon, bright sunlight, clear blue skies, and an ancient peace and quiet. Interestingly, both George and Joy spoke to us about the possibilities of some African animals at risk being bred in remote wilderness areas of Australia and in other countries, but on any scale this would be a threat to already fragile ecological balances.

We read George's detailed reports to the Minister of Tourism and Wildlife and they were a fascinating and invaluable day-by-day record of a pride of lions over several years, particularly charting Christian's successful rehabilitation. In the past both George and Joy's work had been criticized by some for not being "scientific" enough, as they had not methodically recorded information to prescribed formulas. But after living with and observing particular animals over many years and several generations, by keeping diaries and notes, writing books and many letters, they have made the greatest contribution to our documented knowledge about lion behavior.

The lionesses had mated with the wild lions, leaving Christian rather isolated and Tony was trying to get a slightly younger male lion from the Nairobi Orphanage to help ease Christian's loneliness. He may have been the nominal head of a pride, but the lionesses consorted with his enemy, and on his own he could not establish a territory here to raise his own cubs.

Christian was clearly ready to get on with a new stage in his life in the wild, and he had already spent extended periods away, possibly looking for a more suitable place to live. While Christian had survived successfully so far, we realized he may have to move far away, with the likelihood that none of us would ever see him again.

Back in Nairobi, we staged a viewing of *The Lion at World's End* documentary to various people who supported and appreciated the significance of George's work, including the Permanent Secretary, the Minister for Tourism and Wildlife, and the Russian Ambassador to Kenya. Kampi ya Simba was an expensive camp to maintain, and there was no support from Joy, who was behaving predictably and blocking any funding for George's work from the

Elsa Conservation Trust. Bill Travers had moved on to other projects, and was currently working on a documentary with Jane Goodall about her work with chimpanzees. Income from Christian's documentaries helped fund George's work, and various visitors, supporters, and admirers also contributed.

Back in London Tony Fitzjohn visited us with the news that Christian was extremely well, and a rather unusual peace treaty had been brokered between Christian and one of the wild lions. They were not friends, but they roared to each other and left each other alone.

On the other hand, more worrying news was that some Somali tribesmen and their cattle had moved close to the camp. Christian had killed a few of their cattle, and George was very concerned that Christian would get speared in retaliation. As it was illegal to have cattle in this area, the Game Department and police moved them on, but like the poachers who kill many animals for ivory, body parts, hides, and trophies, the Somali and their cattle would continue to create problems for George.

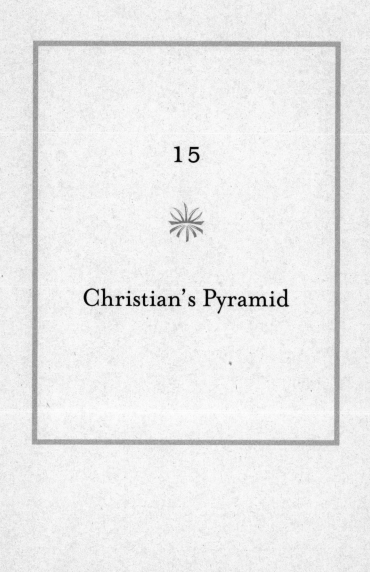

15

Christian's Pyramid

Early in 1973 Christian crossed the Tana River, going north in the direction of the Meru National Park, a much more attractive area and a good hunting ground. In a national park, animals were safer from poachers, hunters, and tribesmen with cattle. Sadly, George finally stopped counting the days and months of Christian's absence from Kora, and he was never seen again. For the next few years we waited for any news. We liked to imagine that he had established a territory and pride of his own a long way away, too far to return to visit George, as he could not leave that pride unprotected. We hoped that he would have lived another ten years and that his descendants live in Kenya today. He had miraculously returned to Africa, adapted quickly, and survived the most dangerous years, and was big and strong. We could not regret anything.

During the first seven years at Kora, George introduced seventeen lions. His rehabilitations were successful but the vicissitudes of life in the wild claimed many lives. Christian's rehabilitation was a complete success. In his autobiography *My Pride and Joy*, George refers to Christian's "pyramid" rather than "pride." Although George had heard Christian mating with wild lionesses on several occasions, he could only assume Christian had progeny and his own biological pride. However, Kampi ya Simba was made up of lions of various ages that George had selected from different sources, and through his knowledge and patience wove a coherent man-made "pyramid" of lions around Christian. Juma and Lisa mated with a wild lion and had cubs, and some of them in turn had cubs. George did not want to import any more lions as he would have created an imbalance of predators in an area where there was little game. He worked on his autobiography and continued documenting his observations of these next generations, including, we noted, that adolescent male lions at Kora were the most dangerous.

Kora was gazetted as a national park in October 1973, which gave George and his lions government protection and official endorsement for his lion rehabilitation program. George viewed Kora as a monument to "the cheerful, mischievous, and courageous young lion from London." George continued to live at Kora until 1989. One day a visitor to the camp offered to go to the airstrip to meet other visitors but the car was attacked on the road by poachers. George heard the gunfire from his camp, and was murdered by the poachers as he rushed to help her in his vehicle.

We were honored to have met George, and we had such gratitude for his loving care of Christian.

We witnessed the extraordinarily deep understanding and communication George had with his lions and their love and trust of him, even allowing him to treat their injuries. Today he would be called a lion whisperer! His documented contribution to the world's knowledge about lions and conservation is immense, and like many others who were influenced by him, we have supported wildlife and conservation causes ever since.

After *Born Free* there was an explosion of interest in Africa and wildlife, and Joy's publisher Sir William Collins went on to publish many important books. These included Jane Goodall's *In the Shadow of Man* (1971), Mirella Ricciardi's photographic classic *Vanishing Africa* (1971), and various other books related to natural history and man's origins, such as Robert Ardrey's *The Territorial Imperative* (1967) and David Attenborough's *Life on Earth* (1979). People like these laid the foundation for today's conservation movements, and Joy was one of the first to articulate the urgency of man's damaging and degrading relationship with the environment, as evidenced by the current forecasts about the effects of climate change.

A very sobering statistic is that the number of lions in Africa today has declined by two-thirds since Christian's time, making George's archive of information invaluable for the future. We are actively supporting related conservation projects, especially through the George Adamson Wildlife Preservation Trust.

John visited Kora by himself in 1973, and over the years has supported and visited other conservation projects in Kenya, Tanzania, and South Africa. He is a Trustee of the George Adamson Wildlife Preservation Trust (GAWPT), and he lectures on their behalf, including at the Royal Geographical Society in London. He works as a journalist and public relations consultant on travel and wildlife. In 2008, he was executive producer of *Mkomazi: The Return of the Rhino,* a film about the relocation of four black rhinos from South Africa to Tony Fitzjohn at Mkomazi in Tanzania. John has been working with GAWPT to revive the Kora National Park, which was virtually abandoned when George was murdered.

Ace returned to Australia, where he has a career as an art curator specializing in Australian Aboriginal and colonial art. In Africa we bought textiles, carvings, beaded necklaces, and artifacts for the first time, and we have both continued to collect art. Influenced by his visits to Africa, Ace wanted to know more about the original Aboriginal inhabitants of Australia. He discovered an extraordinarily diverse and rich artistic tradition and culture with an exciting contemporary expression, but also post-colonial dispossession and much social and economic disadvantage.

With the YouTube-induced revival of interest in Christian, we have enjoyed reliving and reflecting on our time with Christian, looking at photographs, falling in love with him all over again, and missing him. Looking back, we cannot quite believe it turned out so well and we actually succeeded in returning Christian to Africa.

Christian had great charisma, and it is what carried him throughout his life. He was chosen to be sent to Harrods for sale because he was attractive and had an even temperament. We found him irresistible, and against all reason bought him, while we were not tempted by his sister Marta. When Bill Travers first contacted George in Kenya, he described Christian as "a very beautiful lion." Christian starred in his own film. He became George's favorite and friend, and he was popular with people and lions. Kora was established because of Christian, and Christian's successful adaptation ensured that George remained there for nineteen years, and that Kora became a national park.

Forty years later George's work is still continuing, and Christian's magic is again inspiring us to think about the interrelationship of all living creatures, and the urgency of action for wildlife conservation. If everyone touched by Christian's story focused on addressing some of the key issues faced by the global community, what could we achieve together in the spirit of his capacity for love and love of life?

The George Adamson
Wildlife Preservation Trust

The George Adamson Wildlife Preservation Trust was founded in 1980 by a group of George's friends and supporters. Following George's murder by poachers at Kora in 1989, Tony Fitzjohn, who had been George's assistant for eighteen years, became the Field Director of the Trust.

The original chairman of the Trust was the late Dr. Keith Eltringham, lecturer in Applied Biology at the University of Cambridge. The present chairman is Bob Marshall Andrews Q.C. M.P., and the trustees are Alan Toulson and Andrew Mortimer, (all old school friends of Tony's at Mill Hill School in London), Anthony Marrian, a Kenyan friend of George and Tony's, Major Bruce Kinloch MC, a former District Commissioner in Kenya, Chief Game Warden in Uganda, Tanzania, and Malawi, and Brian Jackman, the distinguished wildlife journalist and feature writer for the *Sunday Times*. Additional U.K. trustees are John Rendall, Paul Chauveau, James Lucas, Tim Peet, and Peter Wakeham, all of whom bring relevant skills and experience to the development and well-being of the project. Trusts have also been established in the United States, Kenya, Tanzania, Germany, and the Netherlands.

In 1989 the Royal Geographical Society hosted a reception for GAWPT to mark the launch of The Mkomazi Project in Tanzania.

The Mkomazi Game Reserve in northern Tanzania had become degraded with rampant poaching, burning, hunting and widespread human encroachment. In 1988 the Tanzanian government decided to restore the reserve as a wilderness area. Tony Fitzjohn, in conjunction with GAWPT, was offered the opportunity to work in partnership with the Tanzanian government on a program of rehabilitation. This is a multidiscipline program of habitat restoration, infrastructural development, endangered-species programs for the African wild dog and black rhino, community outreach programs for the villages surrounding Mkomazi Game Reserve, and an environmental education program for school pupils from these villages.

Twenty years later Tony and the network of George Adamson trusts can proudly show that the financial support from generous friends and a number of notable charitable trusts has resulted in the upgrading of Mkomazi Game Reserve to National Park status, a successful rhino sanctuary (the only one in Tanzania), and an ongoing captive breeding, veterinary, and reintroduction program for the African wild dog.

Since George's death in 1989, Kora National Park has degenerated from lack of management, funding, and protection from poaching and illegal grazing. The Trust is currently negotiating with Kenyan Wildlife Services to return to Kora, restore George's camp, and rehabilitate the Park.

George Adamson Wildlife Preservation Trust
16A Park View Road,
London
N3 2JB

For additional information about GAWPT or to make a donation to continue the work of George Adamson, please refer to the following websites;
In the UK: www.georgeadamson.org
In the USA: www.wildlifenow.com